FORMULA JUNIOR

FORMULA JUNIOR
RACING CARS ...remembered

BERNARD COWDREY

PUBLISHERS **BOOKMARQUE** TYPESETTERS
PUBLISHING

Minster Lovell & New Yatt · Oxfordshire

First published 1993
© Bernard Cowdrey 1993

ISBN 1 870519 17 5

British Library Cataloguing in Publication Data
A catalogue record for this book is available from the British Library.

FRONTISPIECE Formula Junior race at Snetterton in 1961. John Fenning in his Lotus 18 leads Bill Bradley in the Midland Racing Partnership Cooper T56. A further three Lotus 18s and David Prophet in a solitary Kieft (2nd from left) follow.

LIMITED EDITION
This book is produced in a limited casebound edition of no more than 998 copies of which this copy is number

853

....

Edited by T. C. Colverson
Set in 10 on 12 point Garamond Book
Disc conversion by Quorum Technical Services · Cheltenham
Typesetting & origination by Bookmarque
Output on a Linotype typesetter by Bookmarque
Published by Bookmarque Publishing · Minster Lovell & New Yatt · Oxon
Printed & bound by Butler & Tanner Ltd · Frome · Somerset

Contents

Acknowledgements

I AM most appreciative for all the help and advice provided by the following people, for without their support this book would not have been completed.

Special thanks must go to Alan Putt, not only for his most valued assistance but also for his important reference compilations which appear at the end of this book—the time and effort put into these lists is obvious.

Many were also able to provide original photographs of the period—my grateful thanks are therefore due to:

Alan Putt Registrar for Formula Junior Cars
Bob Woodward Jnr Vintage Road Racing Monoposto Register – USA
David Lockspeiser Constructor/driver of the ETA
Len Bridge of Deep Sanderson fame
Richard Utley Designer/driver of the Caravelle
Nick Wotherspoon author: *'Lawrie' Bond – The Man & The Marque* HISTORY OF BOND CARS (PUB. 1993)
John Hine
John Narcisi
John Fenning
Rod Tolhurst
Norman Hillwood
Brian Horwood
Fred Scatley
Duncan Rabagliati

Tom Colverson Editor
Roger Ellis
Haymarket Publications
Chuck Dietrich
Stephen Brodrug
Martin Cowell owner of the Northstar
Tim Whiteaway
Gordon L Jolley
Richard M Koehler
Lynton Money
Patrick Benjafield
Alan Fulwood

Finally, to The Monoposto Racing Club, who have organised and supported the Historic Formula Junior Championship Series for over twenty years.

Introduction

IT all started in 1958 when Count Giovanni Lurani's idea of a racing Formula which would act as a single-seater training ground for Italian drivers came to fruition. In Britain we already had this ideal formula in the shape of Formula 3—cars with 500 cc motorcycle engines helping to groom drivers such as Stirling Moss, Peter Collins, and Tony Brooks, all of whom became successful Grand Prix drivers.

For its first year in 1958, Formula Junior progressed very rapidly, mainly in Italy where it was first introduced. It was simply the case of adapting the current National 750 Formula Corse cars to the new Formula.

Who would have thought that the Formula Junior, with such a short International life span would have made such an impact on the world of motor racing, and would revolutionise Formula One so drastically.

Within six years the cars had developed so much from the early designs of 'ladder'-style tubular steel chassis and with front mounted engines to the more sophisticated monocoque chassis with rear engines.

The early years were dominated, as was expected, by the Italian cars. The Stanguellinis-Fiats helped Roberto Lippi win the Italian Championship in 1958, Raffaele Cammarota in 1959, and also in that same year Michael May of Switzerland to win the International Championship.

It was not until 1960 that Britain took an active interest in the Formula, and the first real clash between the British cars and the Italian cars came in the Monaco Junior race in May of that year. As a result of the British designers deciding to opt for the rear-engined designs, this Monaco race was of special interest, not only from a nationalistic point of view but also from the viewpoint of car design. Henry Taylor, driving the rear-engined Cooper T52 BMC of Ken Tyrrell, won the race.

From 1960 the British-designed cars dominated, particularly the works team from Lotus with drivers such as Jimmy Clark, Trevor Taylor, and Peter Arundell—all three drivers progressing on to Formula One, with Clark winning two World Championships.

The teams became 'mini' Grand Prix teams, being very similar in design to the Formula One cars. It was comparatively easy to convert a Junior to a Grand Prix car. One car racing today in Historic races is a product of this work—the Brabham BT6 of John Narcisi which was originally a Junior but later converted to Formula One specifications by the late David Prophet who fitted, amongst other things, a 1500 cc Lotus Ford engine and raced the car in the 1964 South African Grand Prix. Other cars were developed along similar lines including the 1961 Lola Mk 3 of Hugh Dibley. This had the bored out 1340 cc 109E Ford Classic engine fitted.

In 1960 Formula 2 was dropped, so if you were successful in Junior the natural progression would be to Formula One.

The Formula thus became the forerunner to the current Formula Three, albeit with a number of changes over the years. A number of drivers—Jimmy Clark, Trevor Taylor, Pete Arundell as mentioned earlier—went on to Formula One, as did Henry Taylor, John Surtees (who made his four-wheel debut in 1960 at the wheel of the Ken Tyrrell Cooper), Denis Hulme, Richard Attwood, Frank Gardiner, Jochen Rindt—the list is endless.

Introduction

Although the Formula came to an end in Britain at the close of the 1963 season, other countries throughout the world continued. For 1964, Juniors were either converted for the new Formula 2, or for the less powerful Formula 3—cars which became renowned for their famous 'screamer' engines with the single carburetter. In 1964 the Formula made way for the new Formula 2.

1960 *Terrier-Ford*

What a difference 20 years makes—none! Brian Hart's Terrier is pictured (above) at Goodwood in 1961.

The same car is seen again (below) at Brands Hatch in 1981, this time it was driven by Ken Moore.

The Original F.I.A. Formula Junior Regulations

1   DEFINITION

Cars of the Junior Formula are one-seater racing cars, whereof the fundamental elements are derived from a touring car recognised as such by the F.I.A. (Minimum production 1,000 units in 12 consecutive months).

2   GENERAL CHARACTERISTICS

(a)   Minimum wheelbase: 200 cm. (6ft 7¾ins).

(b)   Minimum track: 110 cm. (3ft 7⁵/₁₆ins).

(c)   Maximum width of body: (measured outside) 95 cm (3ft 1½ins).

(d)   Minimum weight: 400 kg (881.8 lb).
The latter weight limit, however, is reduced to 360 kg (793 lb) for cars with a cylinder-capacity of 1,000 cc or less. The above-mentioned weight shall be measured with the car 'in running order', viz. with all accessories required by these regulations but with dry fuel tank(s).

3   MECHANICAL ELEMENTS

(a)   The cylinder-block, including the cylinder-head and cylinders (if the latter are removable) must be those of the engine belonging to a car classed by the F.I.A. in the Touring category.

(b)   The gearbox must be that of an F.I.A.-recognised touring car. Complete freedom is left with regard to the number and staging of gear ratios.

(c)   The braking system and principle (viz. drum-brakes or disc brakes) must remain the same as on the car from which is taken the engine.

(d)   The system and principle of feeding (by carburetter or by injection) must be the same as on the car from which is taken the engine.

(e)   The cylinder-capacities specified in the present regulations may be achieved by modifying the original bore (increase or reduction). No modification of the stroke is permitted.

(f)   The car must have an automatic starter.

4   BODY

The body, open and offering only one seat, shall comprise, around the pilot's seat, an anti-roll bar, protecting him from being crushed should the car turn over. There shall be a protective device against fire as required by the International Sporting Code (Art. 125).

5   SILENCER

The supplementary regulations of the events may provide that an efficient silencer is compulsory.

6   PROHIBITIONS

It is not permitted:

(a)   To use an engine with one or more overhead camshafts.

(b)   To use a self-locking differential.

(c)   To change the number of crankshaft bearings.

(d)   To change the location of the camshaft.

7   FUEL

Only commercial fuel, as defined by the F.I.A. shall be used.

8   CERTIFICATE OF ORIGIN

Every car of the Junior Formula, when arriving at the beginning of an event, shall be equipped with a certificate issued by the national sports authority concerned and stating the origin of its fundamental elements.

Chris Lawrence in the Deep Sanderson (Car 130 – Chassis No. 104) chases an Elva, at the BARC Club Meeting, 27 August 1960 at Oulton Park, on his way to the only victory for the marque (70.15 mph).

Fastest lap was Arthur Mallock (71.92 mph) who finished fourth.

Alexis Mk 1 (GB)

THE first Alexis Formula Junior car was built for the 1960 season—it, however, made only a brief appearance in this country before being shipped off to the United States. The car raced just the once in the UK—at Oulton Park—driven by its Australian co-builder Bill Harris.

In the States the car was raced regularly by Noel Thompson in Vintage events. Today it is owned by Duncan Rabagliati who races it in the current Historic events for Formula Junior cars.

The car is photographed in the collecting area at Mallory Park in 1992, prior to the start of the Historic Formula Junior race in which Rabagliati managed to secure a class win.

The chassis number is HF101 ('HF' being the surname initials of the constructors, Bill Harris and Alex Francis).

An Alexis Mk 2 was built, and successful, but little information materialised—a picture appeared in *Motoring News* 3 August 1961.

SPECIFICATION
Engine: BMC 'A' Series – 998 cc
Chassis: Tubular space frame
(Aluminium body).
Suspension – Front: Triumph Herald,
double wishbone and coil-spring/
damper units. Rear: rigid rear axle
mounted originally on ¼-elliptic leaf
springs (identical to the U2 as they were
produced at the same time)
Transmission: Gearbox – BMC

Alexis Mk 3 (GB)

FOLLOWING the success of the front-engined Alexis Mk 2, Alex Francis and Bill Harris decided to build this rear-engined Formula Junior car for the 1961 season. It was designated the Mk 3, of which only two examples were built.

The cars were run under the name of Team Alexis, and the racing was shared between three drivers: Peter Proctor, Jack Pitcher, and Phil Robinson. The team were quite successful with a win at the Oulton Park Gold Cup Meeting and with Pitcher winning at Cadwell Park.

The Mk 3 was also raced during the 1962 season—its successor not making its début until late in the season at Silverstone on 12 May. The Mk 3 was continually raced during the season, often alongside the Mk 4.

The car depicted is the Mk 3 of Team Alexis (chassis number HF301), photographed at Goodwood during the 1962 BARC Formula Junior Championship when David Prophet drove the car to seventh place behind that regular winning combination, Peter Arundell and the Team Lotus 22.

SPECIFICATION

Engine: 1097 cc Ford 105E tuned by Holbay or Cosworth (dry sump engines were available as an option).
Chassis: Tubular space frame.
Wheels – 13-inch magnesium alloy.
Brakes – Girling discs all round (twin rear discs mounted inboard).
Suspension – Front & rear: wide-based wishbones on shock-absorber/spring units.
Transmission: Clutch – hydraulically operated (diaphragm type with special lining).
Gearbox – Volkswagen housing, 5-speed straight cut gears.
Dimensions: Wheelbase 7ft 5ins   Height 2ft 2ins.
Track 2ft 2½ins   Ground clearance 4ins.

Ausper Type 3 (AUSTRALIA)

AUSTRALIAN Tom Hawkes was the man behind the Ausper which first started as the Tomahawk making its début in October 1960 driven by Peter Jopp. During the winter of that year Hawkes formed Competition Cars of Australia and produced the Ausper T2. However, for 1961 the Type 3 was built and was raced regularly by Count Steve Ouvaroff. Wherever it appeared it impressed—Ouvaroff finishing in a worthy fourth place against strong opposition at the Oulton Park Gold Cup Meeting.

The Ausper Type 3 shown is that of Rod Tolhurst being driven by Roy Drew at the Historic Formula Junior race at Silverstone in September 1990. The inset picture is Roy Drew at Mallory Park in 1992.

SPECIFICATION
Engine: Ford 105E, 1097 cc – tuned by Cosworth. Twin 40DC0E2 Weber carburetters
Chassis: Multi tubular space frame
Wheels – 15-inch Cooper
Brakes – Outboard Alfin drums all round; 10-inch front, 9-inch rear.
Suspension – Front: unequal length wishbones with coil-springs. Rear: universally jointed driveshaft at top wishbone, and lower wishbones with twin parallel radius rods.
Transmission: Clutch – Borg and Beck
Gearbox – Renault 4-speed (modified by Ausper)

Ausper Type 4 (AUSTRALIA)

FOR 1962 Competition Cars of Australia produced the Ausper Type 4: this made its début at Silverstone in May in the hands of John Rhodes.

That same month Rhodes gave the Ausper Type 4 its only win at Brands Hatch but then left the team in July to join Alexis and drive their new Mk 4. Other drivers regularly racing the 'works' cars included Brian Gubby, John Ampt, and American Roy Pike (who reverted back to the older Type 3 for a few races as he much preferred its handling).

The Type 4 was much sleeker in design than its predecessor, with its faired-in mirrors and its 'state of the art' Mini rubber suspension.

The smooth lines of the Type 4 can be seen here when it was pictured in the paddock at Goodwood during 1962 on two different occasions. On the left was at the time of the Whit Monday Meeting, and on the right during August at the BARC Formula Junior Championship. Brian Gubby was the driver at both meetings.

SPECIFICATION

Engine: Ford 105E, 1097 cc (inclined 75 degrees to the right).
Chassis: Tubular space frame with stressed bulkhead at the rear of the cockpit.
Wheels 15-inch pierced alloy.
Suspension – Front: unequal length wishbones with 'Mini' rubber suspension units; Rear: twin parallel radius rods, rectangular top wishbone, Armstrong shock absorbers and 'Mini' rubber suspension units.
Tranmission: Gearbox – Renault 6-speed with transfer box developed by Bill Blydenstein

Bandini (ITALY)

FOR 1960 Bandini built this pretty front-engined Junior which was designed along the lines of the Indianapolis cars of the time and built mainly for the American market. With its 1100 cc Fiat engine, tilted at an angle of 15 degrees to improve carburation and exhaust flow, and with twin Weber carburetters, it promised a top speed of between 132-137 mph.

The car was well-balanced, with the driver seated in a roomy cockpit in the centre of the car. The chassis was the conventional space frame type. Roger Ward of Indianapolis fame drove the Bandini in the Vanderbilt Cup Race on Long Island, New York, in June 1960. As late as 1963, W T Hotchkiss won the front-engined class of the Formula Junior at Sebring.

The picture opposite shows Rod Tolhurst driving his beautiful model of the early front-engined Bandini.

The car on this page is the later rare rear-engined Bandini BFS TIPO PI of which only one example was built. This particular car is seen at Brands Hatch in 1985 when it was raced by Ken Booth.

SPECIFICATION

Engine: Fiat 1100 cc – side-draught 2 Weber 38DCOE1 carburettors.

Chassis: Tubular space frame
Wheels – Amadori magnesium
Brakes – Fiat drum

Dimensions: Overall – Length 11ft 10ins   Height 3ft 6½ins.
Wheelbase 6ft 8ins   Track (front) 3ft 11½ins, (rear) 3ft 9½ins
Ground clearance 4½ins.

BMC (USA)

THE BMC (British Motor Car Distributors Ltd, San Francisco) was designed at the end of 1959 by the experienced ex-hot rodder Joe Huffaker. So successful was its design—during 1960 the car won nine times and had two second places—that by the end of the season some 20 cars had been built. Sometimes referred to as the Huffaker-BMC, this very small front-engined car (having a wheelbase of only 6ft 8ins) was powered by a 998 cc BMC 'A' Series engine and had the conventional tubular space-frame chassis. The car made its début at Stocton, California, in April 1960 when it won first time out in the hands of American Jack Dalton—against imposing opposition of both American and European cars.

Jack Dalton continued to drive the cars regularly throughout 1960.

A rare, but poor picture here of the rear-engined 1961 BMC Mk 2, again powered by the BMC engine with twin-choke Weber 40DCOE carburetter. The car had a Volkswagen 5-speed Hewland gearbox.

Opposite is the Mk 1 BMC resplendent in its American livery.

SPECIFICATION
Engine: BMC 'A' Series – 998 cc – 4 cylinders.
One twin-choke Weber 40DC03 carburetter.
Chassis: Square tubular frame.
Wheels – 13-inch magnesium bolt-on.
Brakes – drum.
Suspension – Front: Wishbones and coil-spring damper units.
Rear: transverse links and twin radius rods and coil-spring damper units.
Transmission: Clutch – Borg and Beck single dry plate.
Gearbox – BMC 4-speed.
Dimensions: Overall – Length 11ft 1in   Height 2ft 5¾ins.
Wheelbase – 6ft 8ins   ground clearance 4¾ins.

Bond (GB)

I HAD always thought that the Lotus 27 was the first monocoque Formula Junior car, but I've now discovered that the front-engined Bond—built as early as the latter part of 1960—had a monocoque chassis made of fibreglass, reinforced with aluminium and steel inserts. There were two cars constructed by this Loxwood-based company, although Lawrie Bond only fully completed one car for competition. The first race for the car was at the 44th Goodwood Members' Meeting held on 11 March 1961, when John Goddard-Watts was given the 'works' drive. Lying in seventh place at the end of the first lap, he was unfortunately to retire with engine problems after three-quarters distance. The Bond then appeared at the Goodwood Easter Monday Meeting, but again it did not to feature in the results.

The Bond was also seen as late as 1963, this time in the hands of Chris Featherstone who raced it in Formula Junior all that season, and then in Monoposto until 1968.

Pictured is the Bond displayed on Stand 25 at the 1961 Racing Car Show, and Featherstone hill climbing his Bond.

SPECIFICATION
Engine: Ford 105E developed by Cosworth – 997 cc. 2 twin-choke Weber carburetters
Chassis: Fibreglass monocoque, reinforced with aluminium and steel inserts.
Wheels – Bond bolt-on
Steering – rack and pinion
Brakes – Girling 9in x 1¾in; Bond drum
Suspension – Front: independent by wishbones and coil-spring/damper units. Rear: Low pivot swing axles with coil-spring/damper units.
Transmission: Clutch – single dry plate
Gearbox – Ford 4-speed and reverse
Dimensions: Overall – Length 11ft 10ins   Width 4ft 4ins
Wheelbase – 7ft 3ins   Track (front) 3ft 10ins, (rear) 3ft 11ins
Ground clearance 4½ins

Brabham BT2 (GB)

THE BT2, Jack Brabham's original single-seater first started life in 1961 as the MRD (Motor Racing Developments) and was raced by the Tasmanian, Gavin Youl. For 1962 it was renamed the BT2 and it is understood that thirteen cars were built. The regular 'works' drivers were Gavin Youl and Frank Gardner (see period photo section, both drivers at Goodwood), ably supported at times by Dennis Hulme. Jo Schlesser did exceedingly well on the Continent wining the French Formula Junior Championship—he won the big race at Montlhèry in May 1962.

Another driver worthy of mention is South African Bob Olthoff, a consistent driver throughout the season in the BMC engined BT2 entered by Team Springbok.

The car shown is Mike Harrison's pictured at Mallory Park during April 1986 with Mike Littlewood at the wheel—he won the 10-lap Historic Formula Junior race.

SPECIFICATION

Engine: Ford – developed by Holbay, 1097 cc
Chassis: Space frame
Wheels – Tauranac designed 13-inch.
Steering – Rack and pinion
Brakes – Girling discs, inboard at rear.
Suspension – Front: Wide-based lower wishbones and short upper wishbones. Rear: two wide-based wishbones. Coil-spring/damper units all round.
Transmission: Clutch – Single plate.
Gearbox – Volkswagen 5-speed.
Dimensions: Overall – Height 2ft 3¼ins   Width 2ft 2ins.
Wheelbase 7ft 6ins   Track (front & rear) 4ft.

Brabham BT6 (GB)

THE fastest Formula Junior car in the World! Not really, this is John Narcisi's ex-David Prophet BT6 which started life as a Junior and was later converted to Formula One specification—the car having competed in the 1963 South African Grand Prix.

The BT6 was built for 1963. Because of the problems Lotus had experienced at the start of the season with the rigidity of the monocoque on their 27, some potential Lotus customers were lost to Brabham.

The BT6 turned out to be a successful car, yet despite this Arundell (in the Lotus) was still just able to win the British Championship. Denis Hulme drove the works car to good effect, while Ian Walker ran Frank Gardner and Paul Hawkins in the familiar yellow and green cars. Gardner won the Prix de Paris and the Chichester Cup, while Hulme had three good British wins and took the Rheims Junior race. As a matter of interest the Ian Walker Brabhams were offered for sale at the end of the season for £1,600 each!

SPECIFICATION
Engine: Ford developed by Holbay – 1097 cc. 2 twin-choke Weber carburetters.

Chassis: Multi-tubular space frame.
Wheels – 13-inch magnesium bolt-on.
Steering – rack and pinion.
Brakes – All outboard, discs all round.
Suspension – Rear: Lower wishbones with parallel radius arms.
Front: Wide-based lower wishbones and short upper wishbones, coil-spring/damper units all round.

Transmission: Clutch – single plate 7¼-inch.
Gearbox – Hewland MkV 5-speed.

Dimensions: Overall – Length 12ft 1in
Width 4ft 8ins
Height (to top of roll bar) 2ft 3ins.
Wheelbase 7ft 6ins.
Track (front) 4ft 2ins (rear) 4ft 1in.

Britannia (GB)

BUILT for the 1960 season, this was John Tojeiro's first ever design for a single-seater car. The majority of Britannias were exported to the United States, and very little is known about the racing achievements of the remaining cars in Europe. Tom Bridger was to have raced a Britannia in 1960 but did not because of engine problems.

The car shown is that of Vivien Ayres which can regularly be seen in Historic Formula Junior events today—the chassis number for this particular car is B3/60.

SPECIFICATION

Engine: Ford 105E – 1098 cc tuned by Bill Basson.

Chassis: Multi-tubular space frame; body by Maurice Gomm.

Wheels – Magnesium 15-inch (later changed to 13-inch).

Steering – Rack and pinion.

Brakes – 9in x 1¾ins Alfin drums all round; outboard at front, inboard at rear.

Suspension – double wishbones and coil-spring/damper units.

Transmission: Gearbox – Volkswagen 4-speed.

Dimensions: Wheelbase 7ft.
Track (front) 3ft 9ins (rear) 3ft 11ins.

Caravelle (GB)

DESIGNED by Richard Utley and built by Bob Hicks, the Caravelle first appeared at the BARC Formula Junior Championship at Goodwood on 20 August 1960 where it finished in an excellent tenth with Bob Hicks at the wheel. Hicks continued to race the Mk 1 for the remainder of the season, and each time he impressed the opposition, always finishing well up in the results.

During the Winter of 1960/1961, the second and third cars were built, each car being a development of the other. Unfortunately the year did not start too well for the team when Richard Utley wrote off the Mk 2 car in torrential rain at Brands Hatch on the Easter Monday. How many of you can recall those terrible conditions on that day, which also caused problems for the Juniors at Goodwood—the race ending in a dead heat between Peter Arundell and Tony Maggs.

The third car made its début at the 1961 Monaco race—the driver was Frank Francis. Bob Hicks again showed good form throughout the next two seasons driving a Mk 3; at the 1961 and the 1962 Goodwood Whit-Monday races he finished in third and second place respectively (Hicks seemed to enjoy that event).

Other Caravelle drivers were 'Dizzy' Addicott and Mike Ghazala.

SPECIFICATION (Mk 1)
Engine: Ford 105E – 997 cc.
Twin 38 DCO Weber carburettors.
Chassis: Multi-tubular space frame.
Wheels – 13-inch magnesium.

Steering – rack and pinion.
Brakes – Lockheed drum brakes, Alfin drums.
Suspension – Front & Rear: Independent by unequal length wishbones and Armstrong spring/damper units (rear: diagonally mounted wishbones).
Transmission: Clutch – Borg and Beck 7¼-inch single dry plate.
Gearbox – Renault 5-speed.
Dimensions: Length 10ft 3ins; Width 4ft 5ins; Height 2ft 10ins.
Wheelbase: 7ft; Track (front) 3ft 10ins, (rear) 4ft 1in.

Condor (GB)

TED Whiteaway of Guildford built this front-engined car for the 1960 season. It had a conventional space frame chassis, and originally it was to have been powered by a Triumph Herald engine; however, this was changed to the Ford 105E unit. Whiteaway himself raced the car in this country and also exported a few Condors to the United States.

For the following season, the Condor S 111 was constructed; this was rear-engined and powered by a 997 cc Ford 105E engine.

Again the chassis was the space frame type, with Whiteaway casting his own 13-inch wheels. Power was transmitted via a modified Renault gearbox and Borg and Beck 7¼-inch single dry plate clutch. Its wheelbase was 7ft 4ins, its length 11ft 6ins and had a height of 2ft 9ins.

Pictured is a rare shot of two front-engined Condors and also the rear-engined 1961 Condor S 111 in action.

Cooper T52 (GB)

IT was the T52 with which John Surtees made his four-wheel début—at Goodwood in March 1960—where he finished second to Jimmy Clark (both were to become future World Champions). The T52, based on traditional Cooper standards, was first raced at the 1959 Boxing Day Brands Hatch Race and was driven by Mike McKee.

Ken Tyrrell ran a team of Coopers throughout the 1960 season and had John Surtees, Henry Taylor, Keith Ballisat, and John Love as his drivers. Unfortunately, they had limited success for they were outclassed by the speed of the Lotus 18—which had the power of the Cosworth Ford engine. However, despite this disadvantage, Henry Taylor managed to win the prestigious Monaco Cup and the Albi Grand Prix, while Denny Hulme also had some success in Europe. Mike Spence regularly drove the Coburn Engineers T52 during 1960.

The car pictured is the very rare ex-Agostini Cooper T52 (which has a Lancia engine) being driven by Rod Tolhurst at Brands Hatch in more recent times.

SPECIFICATION

Engine: Modified BMC 'A' Series – 994 cc, 4 cylinders. 2 SU Ha or 1 twin-choke Weber 45DCOE4 carburetters.

Chassis: Tubular space frame. Wheels – Cooper magnesium bolt-on. Steering – Cooper rack and pinion. Brakes – Lockheed 8-inch. Suspension – Front: independent by unequal-length wishbones, coil-spring/damper units and anti-roll bar. Rear: transverse leaf spring and lower w/bone.

Transmission: Clutch: Borg and Beck 6¼-inch single dry plate. Gearbox: Citroën ERSA 4-speed (Renault optional).

Dimensions: Overall – Length 11ft; Width 4ft 4ins; Height 4ft 4ins. Wheelbase 7ft 2in; Track (front) 3ft 10½ins, (rear) 3ft 10ins.

Cooper T56 (GB)

IT was hardly surprising that following Walt Hansgen's début win for the Cooper T56 at Riverside in November 1960, a number of people made the decision to race the new Cooper in 1961—many with success.

Ken Tyrrell ran the 'semi-works' team, again with Tony Maggs and John Love, achieving 11 major victories between them—including the GP Frontieres and the Lottery Grand Prix. They ran with the enlarged 1098 cc BMC engines.

The Midland Racing Partnership fielded a three-car team on occasions, running with both Ford and BMC engines. Their star driver for 1961 was John Rhodes, who was partnered by Richard Attwood and Bill Bradley.

Other T56s were run by Ecurie Vienne who had two cars for Kurt Bardi-Barry and R Markel, while Bob Gerard also ran a two-car team. In the United States, Ricardo Rodriguez was also successful with a T56.

Rod Tolhurst T56 is pictured, seen at Brands Hatch for the Historic Formula Junior race during August 1983.

SPECIFICATION

Engine: BMC 'A' Series – 994 cc, 4 cylinders.
2 SU H4 or 1 twin-choke Weber 45DCOE4 carburetters.
Chassis: Tubular space frame.
Wheels – Cooper Magnesium bolt-on.
Steering – Cooper rack and pinion.
Brakes – Cooper radially-finned drums, 8-inch diameter, 1½-inch wide shoes.

Suspension – Front & rear: independent by unequal length wishbones, coil-spring/damper units and anti-roll bar.
Transmission: Clutch – Borg and Beck 6¼-inch single dry plate.
Gearbox – Citroën ERSA 4-speed (Renault optional).
Dimensions: Overall – Length 11ft 6ins; Width 4ft 6ins; Height 2ft 7ins.
Wheelbase 7ft 5ins; Track (front) 4ft, (rear) 3ft 11ins.
Ground clearance 4ins.

Cooper T59 (GB)

UNVEILED at the 1961 Racing Car Show, John Cooper produced a lower, more streamlined car for the 1962 season. This time the Coopers were to be powered either by BMC or Ford engines, and were fitted with disc brakes all round. Ken Tyrrell continued to run the official team cars, opting once again for BMC engines, while the Midland Racing Partnership (MRP) chose Cosworth-tuned Ford engines for their Mk 3s.

The Tyrrell 'twins' continued to be John Love and Tony Maggs, although they were joined on occasions by Denis Hulme and Peter Procter—the latter when a Gemini drive was unavailable. MRP kept the services of Richard Attwood (who incidently found the new Ford power to his liking) and Bill Bradley,

while John Rhodes had left the team to join Alexis and ultimately Ausper.

Other Ford-powered cars were raced by Scuderia Light Blue for Bill McCowen, while on the Continent mention should also be made of Kurt Bardi-Barry, Kurt Ahrens Jnr, and Frenchman Jose Rosinki—all of whom achieved success in their similar machines.

SPECIFICATION

Engine: BMC 'A' Series – 1095 cc (some had Ford Cosworth). Twin choke Weber 45DCOE carburetters.

Chassis: Tubular space frame. Wheels – cast magnesium alloy bolt-on.

Steering – rack and pinion.

Brakes — Lockheed discs all round.

Suspension – Front and Rear: wishbones and coil-spring/damper units.

Transmission: Clutch — Borg and Beck, 7-inch diameter.

Gearbox – Citroën 5-speed.

Dimensions: Overall – Length 11ft 6ins; Width 4ft 7ins; Height (to top of roll bar) 2ft 7ins. Wheelbase 7ft 5ins; Track (front) 4ft 2½ins, (rear) 4ft 1¾ins. Ground clearance 4½ins.

Cooper T67 (GB)

THE official 'works' team was once again run by the Tyrrell Racing Organisation, who throughout the Formula Junior era had relied on BMC engines—1963 was no exception. With Tony Maggs joining Bruce McLaren in the Cooper Formula One line-up, the Tyrrell drivers for this last season of Formula Junior racing included Peter Proctor, John Rhodes, Frenchman Jose Rosinki, Chris Amon, and Americans Tim Mayer and Peter Revson.

In addition to this impressive line-up of driving talent, the new Coopers were also driven successfully on the Continent by Kurt Ahrens Jnr and Kurt Bardi-Barry, both drivers gaining wins in their Ford-engined T67s. The Belgian Racing Team also ran two cars for Jean-Claude Franck and 'Elde'. In total some sixteen T67s were built.

Bill Burrows' T67 is shown, which was raced regularly by him in Historic Formula Junior events during the 1980s. This car is in fact the famous ex-Charlie Crichton-Stuart T67, chassis number FJ/12/63.

SPECIFICATION
Engine: BMC – 1098 cc and Ford 1098 cc.
Chassis: Tubular space frame.
Wheels – Magnesium with 5½-inch rims.
Steering – Cooper rack and pinion.
Brakes – Outboard disc brakes all round.
Suspension – Coil-spring, wishbones all round.
Transmission: Gearbox – Citroën, six speed straight cut.

Deep Sanderson (GB)

O NE could easily be forgiven for considering the Deep Sanderson to be an early Formula Vee car in view of the number of Volkswagen components which were used in its construction. Three identical cars were built for 1960 (chassis numbers 101-103), and these became great favourites with the British crowds, racing regularly throughout the country. The drivers were Len Bridge (who races today in the Porsche Challenge), Nobby Smith, Leslie Fagg, Bob Staples, Richard Shepherd-Barron, and the man behind the project himself, Chris Lawrence.

A major win eluded the team—despite Len Bridge's second place, first time out—therefore it was decided to build a new version for the 1961 season.

The new car (chassis no. 104) was ready during mid-1960 and in August of that year Chris Lawrence won at Oulton Park: this was to be the one and only victory for a Deep Sanderson. The 104 was then modified and became the 105, which Len Bridge raced throughout 1962 in its familiar blue livery.

Pictured (car 5) is one of chassis 101-103; a rear view of chassis 104/105, and Len Bridge sitting in chassis 105 (car 123)—which Bridge drove throughout 1962; the chassis was tubular space frame, its alloy body was made by Maurice Gomm, and the wheels were Elva. This was the last of the four Deep Sandersons to be built.

SPECIFICATION

Engine: Ford 105E (developed by Lawrencetune) – 997 cc. 2 twin-choke Weber 40DCOE2 carburetters.
Chassis: Tetrahedron space frame.

Wheels – Deep Sanderson Elektron bolt-on.
Steering – rack and pinion.
Brakes – Front: Alfin drum with 10-inch Girling backing plates. Rear: Girling 9 X 1¾-inch drums.
Suspension – Front: independent Lawrence Link trailing arms.
Rear suspension: swing axle.

Deep Sanderson

Transmission: Clutch – Volkswagen 7⅛-inch single dry plate.
Gearbox – Volkswagen 4-speed, all-syncromesh.
Dimensions: Overall – Length 11ft 1in; Width 4ft 6ins;
Height 2ft 7ins.
Wheelbase 7ft.
Ground clearance 5ins.

Elfin (GB)

THE Elfin was designed and built by Peter Emery, brother of Paul Emery (of Emeryson fame – see page 39). It appeared rather late in the Formula Junior era for a front-engined car. This front-wheel-drive car made its début during the Autumn of 1960, when most constructors had decided by this time that the way forward in the Formula was via the rear-engined route, as had been successfully proven by both Lotus and Cooper.

Two Elfins were built with BMC power and a third was powered by a Ford engine and had a longer wheelbase.

The braking system on the Elfin deserves mention for it was rather unusual: at the front there were four brakes—2 inboard and 2 outboard.

SPECIFICATION

Engine: BMC 'A' Series or Ford 105E.

Chassis: Multi-tubular space frame (fibre glass body).

Wheels – Magnesium alloy, 13-inch.

Brakes – Bimetal alloy turbo finned drum, 8-inch (front) 7-inch (rear) Girling.

Transmission: Gearbox – 4-speed.

Dimensions: Overall – Length 11ft; Width 4ft 4½ins; Height (to top of headrest) 3ft 2ins.

Wheelbase 6ft 7ins. Track – (front and rear) 3ft 11ins.

Elva 100 Series (GB)

FRANK Nichols was one of the few British manufacturers who had the early foresight to realise that the way forward in motor racing was with Formula Junior. As a result he produced one of the most successful cars with the front-engined Elva 100 Series, for it was the first British car (and the only Formula Junior car) to start in the first UK event (April 1959), the first British car to win an International Race, the first mass-produced British car, and lastly it was the car which won that famous Brands Boxing Day event in 1959.

Production continued until mid-1960, with Peter Arundell and Chris Threlfall driving the works cars, while Charlie Kolb won the 1960 American Formula Junior Championship.

The picture of this 100 Series car was taken at Zolder in August 1986, and shows Dieter Crone leaving the pits in the ex-Charlie Kolb car (chassis no. 100/76).

SPECIFICATION
Engine: BMC 'A' Series, modified by Harry Westlake/or DKW 3 cylinder, modified by Mitter.

Chassis: Multi-tubular space frame.
Wheels – magnesium or steel disc 15-inch bolt-on.
Steering – rack and pinion.
Brakes – Lockheed 10-inch drums, inboard at rear.
Suspension – Front: independent by upper wishbones, coil-spring/damper units and lower single arms connected by anti-roll bar. Rear: independent by coil-spring/damper units, lower single arms, fixed length driveshafts and trailing radius arms.
Transmission: Clutch – Borg and Beck single plate. Gearbox – BMC 'A' type.
Dimensions: Overall – Length 12ft 1½in; Width 4ft 4in; Height 3ft 4in.
Wheelbase 7ft 5in; Track (front & rear) 4ft. Ground clearance 5ins.

Elva 200 Series (GB)

IN 1960 Frank Nichols produced a rear-engined car which made its début late in the season at the British Empire Trophy Race held at Silverstone on 1 October. The drivers were American Chuck Dietrich, and Chris Steele. Dietrich finished a credit-

able third in a very wet race behind Henry Taylor and Peter Arundell, both driving Lotus 18s. Twenty '200' Series Elvas were built, the majority powered by the BMC engine, some drivers opting for the Ford 105E unit.

Other drivers of the '200' included Jimmy Blumer, Sir John Whitmore, and David Piper. A frequent competitor at Goodwood during 1961 was George Naylor, driving Mrs B Naylor's green 200—the rear of this car can be seen in the period photographs section of this book.

The Elva 200 Series example pictured on page 35 is Phoebe Rolt's seen at Silverstone on 22 September 1990, when she raced it in the Monoposto Historic Formula Junior Race. Phoebe was 1992 European Historic Single-Seater Champion in her Elva.

SPECIFICATION

Engine: BMC 'A' Series, modified by Rytune – 992 cc. 2 SU 1½-inch HA carburetters.

Chassis: Tubular space frame with stressed undertray. Wheels – 15-inch magnesium bolt-on. Steering – Rack and pinion. Brakes – Lockhed 9-inch diameter hydraulic, inboard at rear. Suspension – Front: independent by unequal-length wishbones, coil-spring/damper units and anti-roll bar. Rear: independent by parallel trailing arms, lower wishbones, fixed-length driveshafts and anti-roll bar.

Transmission: Clutch – 7-inch single dry plate with hydraulic ops. Gearbox – Volkswagen all-synchromesh.

Dimensions: Overall – Length 11ft 1in; Width 4ft 6ins; Height 2ft 5in. Wheelbase 7ft 3in; Track (front & rear) 4ft. Ground clearance 4ins.

Elva 300 Series (GB)

THE very low and streamlined successor to the '200' was the '300' Series which made its début at the 1961 Goodwood Whit Monday Meeting. The picture shows the car in bare metal trim at that same meeting with Keith Marsden trying it out in the Paddock. Chris Meek drove the car in the race but unfortunately he had to retire after hitting the chicane. However, the car was officially unveiled for the 1962 season during December 1961, when it was announced as one of the lowest Formula Junior cars to be built.

Just six cars were built—the first two going to the United States. Drivers of the Elva 300 included Bernie Ecclestone and Chris Ashmore.

Shown on page 38 is Chuck Dietrich, who has driven so well over the years for Elva Cars, (and always a supporter of Elva cars) collects third place in the Monoposto Concours at Mid-Ohio in his own Elva 300. In 1960 Chuck lead a John Davy Trophy Race at Brands Hatch driving a front-engined Elva-DKW—ahead of Jimmy Clark, Peter Arundell, Peter Ashdown, and all other works drivers!

SPECIFICATION
Engine: Ford 1097 cc, tuned by Holbay, Cosworth, or Rytune.
Chassis: Tubular space frame.
Wheels – 15-inch.
Brakes – 9-inch Lockheed drum.

Suspension – Front: Unequal length wishbones. Rear: Parallel trailing arms, lower wishbones and fixed length driveshafts. Coil-spring/damper units all round.
Transmission: Gearbox – Modified Volkswagen 5-speed.
Dimensions: Height 2ft 2ins.

Emeryson (GB)

PAUL Emery built four Formula Junior Emerysons for the 1961 season, all similar to their Formula One counterparts, the only difference being the gauge of the chassis tubing and, of course, the engine.

The drivers were Stan Hart and one Mike Spence who went on to greater things in Grand Prix racing. It was Spence who achieved the one and only significant Emeryson win—the 100-mile Commander Yorke Trophy Race at Silverstone during 1961.

In fact, the car pictured is none other than the same car which was driven by Mike Spence, now owned and raced by Mark Linstone in Historic Formula Junior races.

SPECIFICATION

Engine: Ford 105E – 997 cc, 4 cylinder.
2 twin-choke Weber 38DCO3 carburetters.
Chassis: Multi-tubular space frame.
Wheels – Emeryson magnesium bolt-on.
Steering – Emeryson rack and pinion.
Brakes – Girling 8-inch x 1½-inch drums.
Suspension – Front: independent by unequal-length wide-angle wishbones and coil-spring/damper units. Rear: independent by unequal-length narrow-angle wishbones, coil-spring/damper units and adjustable radius arms.
Transmission: Clutch – Modified Volkswagen 7⅛-inch single dry plate.
Gearbox – Volkswagen 4-speed all-synchromesh.
Dimensions: Overall – Length 12ft 7¼in; Width 4ft 3ins; Height 2ft 8ins.
Wheelbase 7ft 4in; Track (front) 3ft 10ins, (rear) 3ft 9ins.
Ground clearance 4ins.

Envoy (GB)

IAN Raby of 'Puddle-Jumper' fame was the man behind the Envoy; he designed the car himself, which many considered to be very similar in design to the old Formula 3 cars which Raby had raced so well in the past. Sewell and King of Chelmsford carried out the construction work of the Envoy.

The cars were raced throughout the 1960 season—Raby running a 'works' team under the name of the Envoy Racing Team, which consisted of himself, Phil Robinson and Brian Spicer as drivers. Brian Spicer continued to drive the Envoy throughout 1961 although production of the Envoy had (by the end of 1960) ceased, and Ian Raby became involved with the Merlyn Mk 3 during 1961.

Despite the Envoy being marketed in the United States, only a few were made; privateers were able to purchase the car for £850 less engine, or £900 with a standard BMC engine.

The picture is of Brian Spicer taken at Brands Hatch in June 1960.

SPECIFICATION

Engine: Ford 105E – 997 cc, 4 cylinder tuned by Alexander.
2 twin-choke Weber carburetters.
Chassis: Ladder type, tubular frame.
Wheels – Elva light alloy bolt-on.
Steering – rack and pinion.
Brakes – Girling 10-inch drums x 1¾ or 2¼-inch.
Suspension – Front: independent by transverse wishbones, coil-spring/damper units and anti-roll bar. Rear: independent by unequal transverse trailing wishbones and coil-spring/damper units.
Transmission: Clutch – Borg and Beck 7¼-inch single dry plate.
Gearbox – Volkswagen 4-speed all-synchromesh.
Dimensions: Overall – Length 11ft 1in; Width 4ft 2½ins; Height 2ft 9ins.
Wheelbase 7ft 3ins; Track (front) 3ft 10in, (rear) 3ft 9ins.
Ground clearance 4ins.

ETA (GB)

BEARING in mind David Lockspeiser's involvement with flying, I had always assumed that the initials ETA stood for Estimated Time of Arrival. However, I've only recently discovered after all these years that the initials stood for Ecurie Toad Automobiles—named after his house, Toad Hall!

The car was originally an Elva and is believed to have been raced by Peter Jopp. In the photographs shown here—one in the paddock at Goodwood (note Formula Junior Terrier behind the ETA)—the Elva shape can be clearly seen during its first season in 1961. However, for 1962, the car appeared with a much more streamlined and smoother body line. This was achieved by relocating the fuel tank from the tail to just in front of the cockpit, thus allowing for the tail to be reduced considerably. Some 8-inches were taken off the height of the original car, reducing the overall height to approximately 2 feet 6 inches.

The ETA retained most of the similar components found on the original Elvas. The power unit was a BMC 'A' Series engine, tuned by Downton and twin SU carburetters were fitted.

David Lockspeiser drove the car on a regular basis throughout the UK, competing at both Club and National level during 1961 and 1962. It was also seen at a number of hill climb events and at the famous Brighton Speed Trials.

The ETA can also be seen in the period photographs section in this book.

Gemini Mk 2 (GB)

THE Gemini Mk 2 had originally started life in 1959 as the Moorland, then Graham Warner (of the famous Chequered Flag Company) took over the car and renamed it after his birth-sign. The début for the Gemini was the 1959 Boxing Day race at Brands Hatch with Jim Clark behind the wheel—Clark was also making his single-seater début.

Although the majority of Mk 2s were exported to the United States, nonetheless they were regularly seen in this country throughout 1960, with Geoff Duke (of motorcycle fame), Mike Beuttler, and the boss Graham Warner, driving the Chequered Flag cars.

The pictures show David Noble's Gemini Mk 2 'resting' at Oulton Park, July 1991, and a wonderful 'in action' shot overleaf taken by motor racing photographer Fred Scatley, during the Monoposto Racing Club Historic Formula Junior race held at Silverstone in September 1990.

SPECIFICATION
Engine: BMC 'A' Series or Ford 105E.
2 Weber 38DCOE carburetters.
Chassis: Multi-tubular space frame.
Wheels – Elektron 15-inch bolt-on.
Steering – modified Triumph Herald rack & pinion.
Brakes – Lockheed 10-inch drum, inboard at rear.
Suspension – Front: independent by unequal-length wishbones and coil-spring/damper units. Rear: independent strut type with coil-spring/damper units, lower wishbones and fixed-length driveshafts.

Transmission: Clutch – Borg and Beck 7¼-inch single dry plate.
Gearbox – BMC 'A' Series 4-speed.
Dimensions: Overall – Length 11ft 6ins; Width 4ft 2in; Height 3ft.
Wheelbase 6ft 10ins   Track (front) 3ft 11ins, (rear) 4ft.
Ground clearance 4½ins.

Gemini Mk 3A (GB)

FOR 1961 Graham Warner's Chequered Flag Company ran a two car team of Gemini Mk 3As. The Mk 3A was an improved version of the Mk 3 (which had made its début at Brands Hatch the previous August, with Sir John Whitmore at the wheel. The regular drivers were Mike Parkes and Bill Moss, the latter having impressed with drives in his outdated, yet famous, light blue Lotus 18. Other drivers included Graham Warner himself and Bill McCowen, while Geoff Duke had a single drive.

The team's finest hour arrived on 3 June at Brands Hatch when Bill Moss and Mike Parkes completed a fine 1-2 against strong opposition. Other successes included the International début win in March 1961 at Sebring by Charlie Kolb, who went on to another win at Marlboro.

The car pictured is the ex-Parkes Gemini at Zolder in 1986 when it was owned and raced by Rod Tolhurst. The chassis number of this car is MK3-2-61.

SPECIFICATION
Engine: Ford 105E – 997 cc.
2 Weber 38DCOE carburetters.
Chassis: Multi-tubular space frame.
Wheels – Magnesium 4-stud bolt-on.

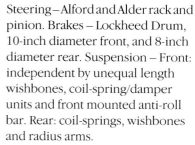

Steering – Alford and Alder rack and pinion. Brakes – Lockheed Drum, 10-inch diameter front, and 8-inch diameter rear. Suspension – Front: independent by unequal length wishbones, coil-spring/damper units and front mounted anti-roll bar. Rear: coil-springs, wishbones and radius arms.
Transmission: Clutch – 8-inch single dry plate. Gearbox – Modified Renault Dauphine.
Dimensions: Overall – Length 11ft 6ins; Width 4ft 9ins; Height 3ft 2ins. Wheelbase 7ft 3ins; Track (front & rear) 4ft 3ins.
Ground clearance 4ins.

Gemini Mk 4A (GB)

BILL Moss drove the Gemini Mk 4 in its début appearance during the 1962 Goodwood Easter Monday Meeting, but while lying in tenth place on lap four he was forced to retire because of a broken oil seal.

Pictured is Peter Procter in the famous 'pencil-shaped' nose Gemini Mk 4A, curbing, with John Fenning in close pursuit in his Lotus 20, at Brands Hatch, 27 May 1962.

Futuristic in design with its side-mounted radiators and

inboard brakes and suspension, much was expected of this car. Sadly neither the Mk 4 nor the Mk 4A reached expectations.

For 1963 George Henrotte took over the running of the 'works' cars—the drivers included John Hine, New Zealander Ross Grenville, Roy Pike, and Sid Fox. The car still had little success, although Roy Pike was able to win the London Trophy at Crystal Palace during September.

Overleaf (p.48) Stephen Bodrug of Ontario in his Gemini Mk 4 leads a pack of Formula Juniors at Mosport, Canada in June 1992. This example is believed to be the Scuderia SSS Repubblica di Venezia car which was driven by Colin Davis, and which made its début at Vallelunga in April 1962.

SPECIFICATION

Engine: Ford 1098 cc developed by Holbay and Cosworth. Dual twin-choke Weber 40DC0E2 carburetters.

Chassis: Multi-tubular space frame.

Wheels – Magnesium alloy 13-inch wide-rimmed.

Steering – Dural rack and pinion.

Brakes – Girling 9½-inch disc, inboard all round.

Suspension – Front: independent by double wishbones. Rear: independent by lower wishbones, single upper arms. Inboard mounted coil-spring/damper units front and rear.

Transmission: Clutch – 8-inch Borg and Beck.

Gearbox – Renault Dauphine casing, 4 or 6 speed.

Dimensions: Overall – Length 12ft 8ins; Height 2ft 8ins. Wheelbase 7ft 11ins; Track (front) 4ft 6ins, (rear) 4ft 5ins.

Hillwood (GB)

NORMAN Hillwood of Lister-Jaguar fame (and still a staunch supporter of Formula Junior racing), built this very attractive one-off Junior for the 1961 season. Racing during that year was shared between the motoring correspondent John Antice-Brown and Norman himself. The car was unusual for British standards because it was fitted with a Fiat engine, rather than the usual BMC or Ford units.

The engine capacity was 1089 cc and was developed by RAM.

It had a tubular space frame chassis, with an alloy body produced by Maurice Gomm. Cooper 15-inch wheels were used and the gearbox was Volkswagen. It was a well-balanced car for it was designed such that when the driver was seated in the car, the weight distribution was 50/50.

The car is pictured with Norman Hillwood behind the wheel at the time of its press anouncement.

Kieft (GB)

THIS was probably the shortest of all Formula Junior racing cars, with a total length of just 9-feet 8-inches. The first Kiefts appeared in the Autumn of 1960—the prototype having a Triumph Herald engine. However, the cars for 1961 reverted to the well-proven Ford 105E units, with Tom Dickson, John Rhodes, and Chris Summers driving the official team cars under the name of Kieft Sports Cars (Rhodes managed a win at Mallory Park). David Prophet, Lionel Mayman, and John Turvey also drove privately-entered cars.

The Kieft was offered for sale in kit form at £1,350.

Fred Edwards drove a Kieft in Historic Formula Junior events for some years, and his car is pictured here in the paddock at Thruxton in May 1982.

SPECIFICATION

Engine: Ford 105E developed by Arden – 997 cc. 2 Weber twin-choke carburetters.
Chassis: Multi-tubular space frame.
Wheels – Kieft Elektron.
Steering – Kieft rack and pinion.
Brakes – Girling 9-inch – outboard front and rear.
Suspension – Front: independent by unequal length wishbones, coil-spring/damper units and anti-roll bar. Rear: independent by wishbones cum radius rods and coil-spring/damper units.
Transmission: Clutch – Borg and Beck 7¼-inch single dry plate.
Gearbox – modified Renault Dauphine.
Dimensions: Overall – Length 9ft 8in; Width 4ft 6ins; Height 2ft 10ins.
Wheelbase 7ft   Track (front and rear) 4ft 1in.
Ground clearance 3ins.

Lola Mk 2 (GB)

THIS was Eric Broadley's first single-seater and was based on the very successful Mk 1 1100 cc sports car. It made its first appearance at the 1959 Boxing Day race at Brands Hatch where, in the hands of Peter Ashdown, it finished in second place. Considered to be the fastest front-engined Junior built—some 19 cars were produced—the majority of which were fitted with Ford 105E engines.

Peter Ashdown and Dick Prior were the 'works' drivers. Richard Fitzwilliam also ran a team of Lolas for such drivers as Juan Manuel Bordeau (Fangio's protégé), Mike Anthony, and John Whitmore, while Team Speedwell had a BMC-engined car for Dennis Taylor. Alan Rees and Hugh Dibley also ran their own cars.

The Lola pictured is at Zolder in 1986, owned by Rodney Tolhurst, and is understood to be the car which was driven by Peter Ashdown—the chassis number is BRJ 13.

SPECIFICATION

Engine: Ford 105E developed by Lola – 997 cc, 4 cylinder.
2 Weber 40DCOE2 carburetters.
Chassis: Tubular space frame.
Wheels – Magnesium bolt-on.
Steering – Lola rack and pinion.
Brakes – Lockheed 9-inch diameter with Alfin drums, inboard at rear.
Suspension – Front: transverse wishbones and coil-spring/damper units. Rear: unequal length transverse wishbones and coil-spring/damper units.
Transmission: Clutch – 7¼-inch single dry plate. Gearbox – modified BMC 'A' Series – 4 speed.
Dimensions: Overall – Length 10ft 8ins; Width 4ft 4ins; Height 3ft.
Wheelbase 6ft 10ins; Track (front) 3ft 9ins, (rear) 3ft 9½ins.
Ground clearance 4½ins.

51

Lola Mk 3 (GB)

THE concept looked right: rear-engined, futuristic design, powered by Ford—yet not one of the Lola Mk 3s produced achieved a major Formula Junior victory during 1961. The Lola Mk 3 was the first car to be designed from scratch with dry-sump lubrication.

Lola Equipé ran a team of three cars for Peter Ashdown, John Hine, and Dick Prior—the team starting with 997 cc Ford engines but later adopting the 1096 cc units. Dennis Taylor did well with his own entry, while Scuderia Light Blue had either Hugh Dibley or Dizzie Addicott as driver, the latter winning at the Goodwood Members' Meeting in July 1961.

The Scuderia Light Blue car is pictured at the 1961 Goodwood Whit Monday Meeting when it was due to be driven by Hugh Dibley. In October of that same year the car ran in a Formula One race at Brands Hatch with a bored out Ford 109E

1340 cc Classic engine—again the driver was Hugh Dibley: he finished in ninth place.

SPECIFICATION

Engine: Ford 105E developed by Super Speed – 997 & 1096 cc. 2 Weber 40DCOE2 carburetters.

Chassis: Tubular space frame.

Wheels – Magnesium bolt-on.

Steering – Lola rack and pinion.

Brakes – Lockheed 9-inch diameter with Alfin drums, inboard at rear. Suspension – Front: transverse wishbones and coil-spring/damper units. Rear: unequal length transverse wishbones & coil-spring/damper units.

Transmission: Clutch – 7¼-inch single dry plate.

Gearbox – modified Volkswagen all-synchromesh.

Dimensions Overall – Length 12ft; Width 4ft 7ins; Height 2ft 10in. Wheelbase 7ft 4ins; Track (front) 4ft 1in, (rear) 4ft. Ground clearance 3½ins.

Lola Mk 5 (GB)

THE Lola Mk 5 was produced for 1962, and updated as the Mk 5A for the following season. During these two years only a small number of cars were built. Ron Harris took over the Lola Equipé during the middle of the 1962 season with John Fenning and John Hine as drivers.

Mention should be of Dennis Taylor who drove his own car, again so effectively, until his sad death during the first heat of the Monaco Junior Race in June 1962. A very sad loss.

In 1963 the Midland Racing Partnership ran the 'works' cars and with drivers such as Richard Attwood, David Hobbs and Bill Bradley, they gained reasonable results—culminating in Attwood winning the Monaco Junior Race. Hugh Dibley drove the Scuderia Light Blue car (see period photograph section), Alan Rees for Roy Winkleman, while Andrea de Adamich, Piko Troberg, and Eric Offenstadt all did well on the European circuits.

One English driver who achieved success in Europe driving his privately-entered Lola was David Hitches: in 1962 he won the Lake Garda race. The photograph here is of this same car seen many years later in 1987 at Silverstone when it was driven by Alan Baillie.

SPECIFICATION

Engine: Ford 105E – 1097 cc, Cosworth or Holbay tuned.
Chassis: Tubular steel space frame.
Wheels – 13-inch magnesium alloy.
Steering – rack and pinion.
Brakes – 9¼-inch Girling disc brakes.
Suspension – Coil-spring/damper units all round, inboard at front, outboard at rear. Paired radius arms all round, front: top wishbone, rear lower wishbones.
Transmission: Clutch – Diaphram spring.
Gearbox – Hewland Mk 4.
Dimensions: Overall – Length 12ft.
Wheelbase 7ft 8ins.

Lotus 18 (GB)

THIS was Colin Chapman's first rear-engined Lotus, and probably the car which made the most impact on Formula Junior racing.

It was built for the 1960 season and made its début at the famous 1959 Boxing Day race at Brands Hatch—Alan Stacey behind the wheel: he finished fourth, behind two Elvas and Ashdown's Lola.

Throughout 1960 the Team Lotus cars of Jimmy Clark and Trevor Taylor totally dominated the racing, and later on in the season Peter Arundell joined them from the Elva camp. Mention should also be made of Mike McKee who did very well in the Jim Russell 18. One hundred and twenty-five Lotus 18s were produced in total.

The picture shows John Fenning driving his Lotus 18 on the limit at Silverstone during 1961. Note daylight under the front offside wheel.

SPECIFICATION

Engine: Ford 105E developed by Cosworth – 997 cc, 4 cylinder. 2 twin-choke Weber 40DCOE9 carburetters.

Chassis: Multi-tubular space frame.
Wheels – Magnesium bolt-on.
Steering – rack and pinion.
Brakes – Lockheed 9ins x 1¾ins, all outboard.
Suspension – Front: unequal-length wishbone and coil-spring/damper units. Rear: independent by single lower wishbone, fixed length articulated drive shaft and coil-spring/damper units.

Transmission: Clutch – Ford 7¼-inch single dry plate.
Gearbox – Modified Volkswagen, all synchromesh.
(Renault gearbox optional).

Dimensions: Overall – Length 11ft 3ins; Width 4ft 8ins; Height 2ft 10ins.
Wheelbase 7ft 6ins; Track (front) 4ft 1in, (rear) 3ft 11ins.
Ground clearance 4ins.

Lotus 20 (GB)

UNVEILED at the 1961 Racing Car Show as the successor to the Lotus 18, the Lotus 20 (with its smoother lines and smaller frontal area) looked every part the potential winner. The 'works' drivers, Trevor Taylor and Peter Arundell, ably supported by Mike McKee, dominated the 1961 season.

Then in 1962, John Fenning, driving the Ron Harris Lotus 20—and pitched against far more up-to-date competition—became the find of the season: Fenning went on to join Ron Harris's Team Lotus with the Lotus 27s for 1963.

In all some one hundred and eighteen Lotus 20s were produced.

The Lotus 20 shown here is of special interest for it is believed to be one of the prototypes with an all-aluminium body, as opposed to the fibreglass body of production models. The car is pictured at Brands Hatch in June 1990 where it was driven by Fred Boothby.

SPECIFICATION

Engine: Ford 105E developed by Cosworth – 997 cc, 4 cylinder. 2 twin-choke Weber 40DCOE9 carburetters.

Chassis: Multi-tubular space frame.
Wheels – Magnesium bolt-on.
Steering – rack and pinion.
Brakes – Girling 8in x 1½in, inboard at rear.
Suspension – Front: unequal-length wishbone and coil-spring/damper units. Rear: independent by single lower wishbone, fixed length articulated drive shaft and coil-spring/damper units.

Transmission: Clutch – Ford 7¼-inch single dry plate.
Gearbox – Modified Volkswagen all-synchromesh.
(Renault gearbox optional).

Dimensions: Overall – Length 11ft 7ins; Width 4ft 9ins; Height 2ft 8ins.
Wheelbase 7ft 6in; Track (front) 4ft 1in, (rear) 4ft.
Weight 805 lbs. Ground clearance 3¾ins.

Lotus 22 (GB)

LOTUS continued to keep up the pressure on it's competitors by producing the Lotus 22 for the 1962 season. With Trevor Taylor moving up to Formula One it was now the turn of Peter Arundell to take the lead role for Team Lotus. This he did admirably, for he enjoyed 18 wins and 3 second places from 25 starts. As Mike Mckee had retired, Arundell was supported by Alan Rees and Bob Anderson, while Mike Spence challenged with the Ian Walker car. Most Lotus 22s were fitted with the Ford Cosworth engine, although the 'Geki' car (which helped him to win the Italian Championship for that year) was powered by a DKW unit. 77 Lotus 22s were built.

Brian Horwood's Lotus 22 is pictured at Mallory Park in 1992. Finished in the same colours of the period, this is the ex-André Baldet car which he raced in both Formula Junior (1963) and Formula Three (1964). It was later used successfully by Mike Cataroche in Guernsey hill climb events, and with this car he became the Island's hill climb champion.

The Lotus 22 continued as a Formula 3 car in 1964 and the chassis was revised to produce the Lotus 51 Formula Ford.

SPECIFICATION
Engine: Ford 105E developed by Cosworth – 1098 cc.
2 twin-choke Weber 40DCO carburetters.
Chassis: Multi-tubular space frame.
Wheels – Magnesium bolt-on.
Steering – rack and pinion.
Brakes – Girling discs all round, 9ins x ⅜in.
Suspension – Front: unequal-length wishbone and coil-spring/damper units. Rear: independent by single lower wishbone, fixed length articulated drive shaft and coil-spring/damper units with a top link.
Transmission: Clutch – Borg and Beck. Gearbox – Hewland Mk 6, 5 speed.

Lotus 27 (GB)

FOR 1963 Lotus produced its first monocoque Formula Junior car and although it was regarded to be the ultimate in design, at first there were serious difficulties resulting from its lack of rigidity; this was caused by the construction being a combination of aluminium and fibreglass and, because of these difficulties, a number of potential customers decided to opt for the Brabham BT6. However, once the rigidity problem was resolved—by the fitting of an all-aluminium monocoque—Peter Arundell, driving the Ron Harris Team Lotus car, was still able to win the British Championship. His regular team-mates for the year were John Fenning, Mike Spence, and John Hine. On occasions Peter Procter and Frenchman Jean Vinatier enjoyed a 'works' drive. The latter won at Nogaro in August driving the Ford-France car.

Other Lotus 27 drivers of note included Italian Bruno Deserti (entered by Scuderia St. Ambroeus), Jo Schlesser (for the Ford-France team), and the privately-entered Belgian, Mark de Boe.

SPECIFICATION

Engine: Ford 105E developed by Cosworth – 1098 cc. 2 twin-choke Weber carburetters.

Chassis: Monocoque – originally aluminium/fibreglass, later changed to all aluminium.
Wheels – 13-inch bolt-on magnesium.
Steering – rack and pinion.
Brakes – outboard discs all round.
Suspension – Front: double wishbone (top boxed in) and Lotus inboard spring and damper units. Rear: lower wishbone with paired tubular radius arms, coil-spring/damper units outboard

Transmission: Gearbox – Hewland Mk IV, 5-speed based on Volkswagen gearbox.

Melkus-Wartburg (E GERMANY)

HEINZ Melkus built around half-a-dozen of these rare rear-engined cars, which were successful in their home country of East Germany and in other 'Iron Curtain' countries, although they did occasionally venture across the border into West Germany; in 1960, Willy Lehmann won at Hockenheim. Then at the famous Nürburgring event on 16 October 1960 (when John Harwood won in the Mallock U2), Melkus-Wartburgs finished in third, fourth, fifth and sixth positions—Freider Raedlein, Heinz Melkus, Willi Krenkel and Siegman Bunk in that order respectively.

The Melkus was propelled by the powerful little Wartburg two-stroke, three-cylinder engine—similar to its neighbour the West German DKW unit.

SPECIFICATION
Engine: Wartburg 3 cylinder – 980 cc.
Chassis: Tubular space frame.
Wheels – pressed steel.
Steering — Wartburg AWE.

Brakes – Wartburg AWE.
Suspension – Front: double wishbones with coil-spring/damper units, Rear: de Dion coil springs and de Dion axle.
Transmission: Clutch – single dry plate.
Gearbox – Wartburg AWE, 4 forward speeds. Final drive by chains to halfshafts.
Dimensions: Wheelbase 7ft ½ins; Track (front and rear) 4ft 2½ins.

Merlyn Mk 3 (GB)

MERLYN first entered Formula Junior racing in 1960 with the Mk 2—this was a front-engined car driven by Peter Pilsworth. The Mk 3 was built in 1961, and with the earlier cars being exported to the United States it was not until the 1961 Boxing Day race at Brands Hatch that the potential of the Merlyn was noted. At that meeting the tremendous performance by Ian Raby in his Mk 3 will always be remembered; he started last on the grid because of clutch failure but proceeded to overtake every car in fourth gear, reaching fourth place—unfortunately to spin at Bottom Bend. Raby continued to race the car throughout the 1962 season.

Other Merlyn Mk 3 drivers included the famous father and son team of André and Teddy Pilette, racing under the Equipé Nationale Belge banner. André Pilette finished second in the 1962 Benelux Cup Race.

The Merlyn Mk 3 shown is the Ian Raby car (owned by Brian Taylor) and is pictured in the paddock at Brands Hatch in 1981. I photographed the same car at Goodwood in 1961 and this can be seen on page 80 of this book. 16 Merlyn Mk 3s were built (Raby's was the fifteenth car).

SPECIFICATION

Engine: Ford 105E – 1098 cc Cosworth- or Holbay-tuned. (The Ian Raby car had the modified Ford engine taken from the Raby Cooper used in 1961).

Chassis: Multi-tubular space frame.

Wheels – Merlyn cast magnesium.

Steering – Rack and pinion.

Brakes – Discs all round, inboard at rear.

Suspension – Front: Double wishbones and coil-spring/damper units. Rear: Single lower wishbones and fixed-length drive shafts.

Transmission: Clutch – Volkswagen.

Gearbox – Volkswagen 5-speed.

Dimensions: Overall – Length 11ft; Width 2ft 6ins. Wheelbase 7ft 5ins; Track (front) 3ft 11ins, (Rear) 4ft.

Merlyn Mk 5 (GB)

THE Merlyn Mk 5 made its début at the 1962 Boxing Day race at Brands Hatch, when Jonathan Williams driving the 'Merlyn Racing' car finished in a worthy fifth place.

Williams continued to drive for the works team during 1963, but unfortunately he crashed badly during the Monaco Grand Prix. For the 1963 British Grand Prix meeting John Rhodes drove the Mk 5.

Once again the Belgian André Pilette supported the Merlyn camp and drove regularly on the Continent in his Mk 5 throughout 1963.

The Merlyn Mk 5 pictured is at Oulton Park in July 1991 where driver Alf Skeels won the Monoposto Formula Junior race.

SPECIFICATION

Engine: Ford 105E – tuned by Cosworth.
Chassis: Multi-tubular space frame (fibre glass body).
Wheels – Merlyn cast magnesium.
Steering – Rack and pinion.
Brakes – Girling hydraulic discs, outboard all round.
Suspension – Front: Unequal length wishbones; coil-spring/damper units front and rear. Rear: lower and upper wishbones, sliding half shafts and forward radius rods.
Transmission: Clutch – 7¼-inch diaphragm.
Gearbox – 5-speed.
Dimensions: Overall – Length 12ft.
Wheelbase 7ft 6ins; Track (front and rear) 4ft 4ins.

Moorland (GB)

THE Halson, Elva, and the Moorland were the first British Formula Junior cars to be built during the early part of 1959. The Moorland in particular had a very short life—in fact, it raced only on the one occasion, at Brands Hatch in August 1959. Graham Warner was intending to drive the car on that day but due to problems with traffic on his return from the Continent, Ian Raby had to be drafted in at the last moment. Raby drove the car to a fifth place: the first Formula Junior car home.

After this, Graham Warner (of the Chequered Flag Company) decided to purchase Moorland Cars of Southall. He retained the services of the designer Les Redmond, and changed the name of the car to that of the Gemini Mk 2 (see page 43).

The car next appeared, as the Gemini Mk 2, at the 1959 Boxing Day race at Brands Hatch with Jimmy Clark making his single-seater début. It had been originally intended that Chris Bristow would have driven the first production model of the Moorland in 1959.

The Moorland shown on this page was imported into the USA by Joe Morris Jnr who campaigned the car throughout 1961.

SPECIFICATION Engine: BMC 'A' Series – tuned by Speedwell. Chassis: Multi-tubular space frame (Alloy body). Brakes – Lockheed 8-inch drum (outboard at rear, inboard at front). Suspension – Front: unequal length wishbones. Rear: single lower wishbones and radius arms and coil-spring/damper units all round.

Northstar (GB)

ALTHOUGH construction of the Northstar began in 1960, the car was not seen at the circuits until the 1962 season. Then A P ('Bill') Belcher raced the car regularly at both Club and National level, right the way through until the end of the Formula Junior era.

Ron Robinson built the car, affectionately known as 'FRED' (which stood for Ford Rear-Engined Device). It was somewhat unusual in that it ran on wire wheels (taken from a Lotus 11) instead of the usual magnesium bolt-on versions. The Northstar was rear-engined and fitted with a Ford Cosworth unit; the power was transmitted through a Volkswagen gearbox with the help of a Ford clutch. The aluminium body enveloped the space frame chassis—Alfin drum brakes were fitted all round.

The picture shows Bill Belcher leading David Lockspeiser (in the ETA) at Silverstone during a Formula Junior race in 1962.

After the demise of Formula Junior, the car was fitted with a 1500 cc supercharged engine and competed in Formula Libre races.

Always regarded as an attractive car, it can still be seen at hill climb events in the hands of its present owner Martin Cowell.

SPECIFICATION
Engine: Ford Cosworth.
Chassis: space frame (alloy body).
Brakes – Alfin drum.
Transmission: Clutch – Ford.
Gearbox – Volkswagen.
Dimensions: Wheelbase 7ft 7ins; Track (front) 55ins, (rear) 56ins.

Osca (ITALY)

DESIGNED by the Maserati brothers, the initials OSCA stood for Officine Specializata Costruzione Automobili.

The Osca helped Colin Davis, the Italy-based Englishman, to win the International Championship in 1960 (he also drove a Taraschi and a Stanguellini). A number of Oscas were exported to the United States where it also proved to be successful. Unlike the Stanguellini, the Osca had the cockpit offset to the right.

Other OSCA drivers included Ludovico Scarfiotti (who finished fourth at Pescara in 1960), and Ricardo Rodriguez in the United States.

The car depicted is Kurt Sommer's, seen at Zolder in 1986.

SPECIFICATION

Engine: Fiat 1089 cc – 4 cylinder.
Twin sidedraught Weber 40DCO carburetters.
Chassis: Ladder type tubular frame.
Wheels – Amadori bolt-on cast alloy.
Steering – rack and pinion.
Brakes – 2 leading shoe 10-inch hydraulic drum brakes with transmission handbrakes.
Suspension – Front: independent by twin wishbones with coil-sprint/damper units. Rear: live axle with coil-springs and telescopic dampers.
Transmission: Clutch – single dry plate.
Gearbox – Fiat 4-speed.
Dimensions: Wheelbase 6ft 7ins; Track (front) 3ft 10½ins (rear) 3ft 9ins.
Ground clearance 4¾ins.

Stanguellini (ITALY)

IT was a natural progression for Vittorio Stanguellini to develop his Formula Corse cars to probably what were the most succesful Formula Junior cars to be built in the early years of Formula Junior racing.

Designed by Ing Massimino and tested by Fangio at Modena the car had to be a success. The cars dominated racing throughout Europe in 1958 and 1959: Roberto Lippi became the Italian champion in 1958, with Cammarota champion in 1959, and Michael May winning the international championship, also in 1959.

Other drivers of Stanguellinis included Wolfgang von Trips, Ritchie Ginther, Lorenzo Bandini, and Fangio's protégé Juan Manuel Bordeau.

The Stanguellini met its 'Waterloo' during 1960 with the advent of the rear-engined British Juniors—in particular at the first major meeting, the Monaco Junior Race, won by Henry Taylor in the Tyrrell Cooper. Approximately 150 Stanguellinis were built. Few of them raced in Britain, although Ron Carter—who had an agency for Italian cars—raced one during 1960; this being regarded as the 'show car'.

The Stanguellini pictured is the ex-Brian Horwood car, painstakingly restored by him over many years to the beautiful condition it is found in today, now owned and raced by Martin Bunn. The venue Brands Hatch, Druids Hill Bend, with Frank Tiedeman behind in his Lotus 22.

SPECIFICATION

Engine: Fiat 1100 – 1089 cc.
2 Weber twin-choke DCO3 carburetters.
Chassis: Multi-tubular.
Wheels – Borrani knock-on, wire spoked.

Steering – Worm and roller.
Brakes – Fiat 9.8-inch drums, inboard at rear.
Suspension – Front and Rear: independent by unequal-length wishbones and coil-springs, rear included radius rods.
Transmission: Clutch – Single dry plate.
Gearbox – 5-speed
(4-speed box optional).
Dimensions: Overall – Length 11ft 9ins; Width 4ft 6ins; Height 3ft 5ins.
Wheelbase 6ft 8ins; Track (front & rear) 4ft.
Ground clearance 4½ins.

TCA (W. GERMANY)

THE Ferrari Grand Prix driver, Wolfgang von Trips, was the man behind the little-known TCA, with Valerio Colotti the designer. The constructors of the car were Tec Mec in Italy, and the engine tuners were Mitter—famous for their highly-developed DKW engines. The car therefore implied great potential, but unfortunately did not live up to its reputation.

TCA stood for 'Trips-Colotti-Automobili'. Von Trips himself was involved with some of the testing of the car and it was his protégé, Hans Stausberg, who regularly drove the TCA during the first season of 1960.

SPECIFICATION
Engine: DKW tuned by Mitter – 3 cylinder. 3 carburetters.
Chassis: Tubular space frame. Wheels – Knock-off Amadori. Steering – rack and pinion. Brakes – drum all round. Suspension – (front and rear) independent by lower transverse wishbones and upper transverse leaf spring.
Transmission: Clutch – single dry plate. Gearbox – modified Auto Union 1000, 5-speed.
Dimensions: Wheelbase 7ft 2ins; Track (front) 3ft 11ins, (rear) 4ft ½in.

Terrier (GB)

MAKING its début at the 1960 Goodwood Easter Monday Meeting (The Chichester Cup Race), the Terrier—designed by Len Terry—achieved reasonable success at both Club and National level, bearing in mind the car was completed in just three-and-a-half months. Designated the Terrier Mk 4, only three cars were built.

Brian Hart developed the engine, and it was the only Formula Junior car to have a downdraught cylinder head. However, in 1961 the engine was replaced by the more conventional side-draught version, and Brian Hart himself continued to drive the car with some credit gaining a sixth place at the Goodwood Easter Meeting, followed by a second place at the Whit Monday Meeting at that same circuit.

The Terrier shown is the same ex-Brian Hart car, at Zolder, August 1986, and now owned and successfully raced throughout Europe in Historic Formula Junior events by Lawrence Suffryn. The chassis number of this car is 5/1 which suggests, (after a severe crash at Oulton Park towards the end of the 1960 season), that the intention was to rebuild the car as the first in the line of Mark 5 Terriers.

SPECIFICATION

Engine: Ford 105E – 998 cc.
Twin downdraught Weber carburetters.
Chassis: Multi-tubular frame.
Wheels – steel alloy.
Steering – Rack and Pinion.
Brakes – Cast iron drum.
Suspension – Front: double wishbones & inclined coil-spring/damper units. Rear: lower wishbone and coil-spring/damper units.
Transmission: Gearbox – Austin A35, 4-speed.
Dimensions: Wheelbase 7ft; Track (Front & Rear) 4ft.

U2 (GB)

ARTHUR Mallock built two Formula Junior cars, designated the Mallock Mk 2, and acquired good results for such a low budget car. The most famous win was at the Nürburgring in 1960 when John Harwood brought the car home to victory. It is believed that in an effort to finance his motor racing Harwood ate beetroot sandwiches for six months! For the Rheims race of that same year he was seen driving to the circuit in the actual race car. Mallock himself competed in his astonishing U2 in Britain, and on one occasion beating a host of Lotus 18s at Silverstone! Harwood continued to race his U2 for some time, and with success, for a noteworthy fifth place at Nürburgring in 1962 was gained against far more modern machinery.

For 1962 Arthur Mallock converted one of the Formula Junior U2s for the 1172 Formula and in so doing went on to win the Championship!

The cars pictured are understood to be the same U2s which Mallock and Harwood raced—car 27 is still being entered today by Mike Harrison in Historic events, while car 29 is the only other Mallock U2 Formula Junior, pictured here in the early nineteen-eighties with Alan Baillie at the wheel—after winning at Zandvoort.

The U2 is powered by a front-mounted Ford engine and has a ladder-type chassis, while the rather basic suspension comprises of a Ford swing axle for the front and a rigid rear axle mounted on quarter elliptic leaf springs.

Volpini (ITALY)

VOLPINI was already well known in International motor racing when he decided on building a Formula Junior car for 1958. And with Lurani as consultant, and Columbo (designer of the Alfa Romeo 158 and early Ferraris) as designer, the car promised tremendous potential. However, this was not to be, for although it had an estimated top speed of 130 mph, nonetheless it was still outpaced by the might of the Stanguellinis.

The car was redesigned for 1959 (as seen here), and during that season Lorenzo Bandini drove the car and finished in fourth place in the Monaco Junior Grand Prix at Cemenatico, and also fourth at the final Vallelunga race of that year.

Zanarotti also drove the Volpini—he finished in second place in the famous Cortina Ice races in 1960.

SPECIFICATION

Engine: Fiat 1089 cc – 4 cylinder.
Twin sidedraught Weber 40DCO3 carburetters
Chassis: Ladder type tubular frame.
Wheels – bolt-on alloy disc.
Steering – worm and peg.
Brakes – Fiat 1100/103 Brakes with Alfin drums.
Suspension – Front: independent by unequal length wishbones, combined coil-spring/damper units and forward mounted anti-roll bar. Rear: live axle with coil-springs, radius rods and telescopic dampers.
Transmission: Clutch – single dry plate.
Gearbox – Fiat 4-speed.
Dimensions: Overall – Length 11ft 1¾ins; Height 3ft 3¼ins.
Wheelbase 6ft 10½ins; Track (front) 4ft ½in, (rear) 3ft 11ins.
Ground clearance 5½ins.

Yimkin (GB)

SIMILARLY to the Mallock U2 mentioned previously, there were only two Formula Junior Yimkins constructed, despite much publicity for it in the United States. The car was basically the popular Yimkin 1172 sports car, for by simply removing its cycle mudguards and headlights the car became eligible for Formula Junior racing!

Constructed by Yimkin Engineering, situated in south west London, the car had a BMC 'A' Series (998 cc) engine and a multi-tubular chassis. It could be seen regularly during 1960 at both Club and National level being driven by South African Clive Puzey.

The car shown in the two photographs is that of Ed Glaiser's, seen at Donington in July 1983.

The other Formula Juniors

This section of the book provides a brief description of the remaining British Formula Junior racing cars, including a number of foreign chassis, raced during the 1959 to 1963 era. For completeness, mention should also be made of four British cars for which there appears to be scant information—they are:

Landar (GB)

I saw it race at Castle Combe in 1962.

Fafnir (GB)

I know it raced in Formula 3 in 1964.

Longbacon (GB)

Did it ever race?

Fairthorpe (GB)

This was entered in a race at Silverstone, by Fairthorpe Ltd, on 30 April 1960.

Apache (USA)

An early American Formula Junior car built in 1960, front engined, and powered either by a Simca, Peugeot, or MG engine.

Bennett (GB)

Derek Bennett of Chevron fame built this 'one-off' front-engined Formula Junior car which he raced during the 1960 season. Ford engined, it made its début at Oulton Park in May 1960.

CMB (GB)

This was a rear-engined car designed by John Tilden which had a transverse mounted BMC engine.

Cheetah (GB)

A rear-engined car (pictured) which was later converted to the 1964 Formula 3 specifications.

Raced during the Formula Junior era as H M Slater's Special.

Cheetah

Cooper Raeburg (GB)

Known also as the Raeburg, this car was built up from Cooper 500 parts, including the suspension, but had its own designed tubular space frame chassis. It was raced during 1960 and in 1961 by Peter Belton. The car was built by Aberg Engineering and had a Downton tuned BMC engine.

Dagrada (ITALY)

One of the early Italian Juniors, this front-engined car was powered by a Lancia V4-cylinder engine. The drivers included Juan Manuel Bordeau (Fangio's protégé), and in 1960 Giancarlo Baghetti, who the following year went on to drive the 'Sharknose' Ferrari Tipo 156 and to win his début race: the Syracuse Grand Prix.

De Sanctis (ITALY)

Unusual, in that this was an rear-engined car—the trend in Italy at the time was for the front-engine design. The car was powered by the Fiat engine. It had a ladder-type frame chassis with an aluminum body. In 1960 the cars were driven by Roberto Lippi and Antonio Maglione

Lucien De Sanctis later built Ford engined cars which were driven by Colin Davis and Massimo Natili in 1962, and Odoardo Goroni and 'Geki' in 1963.

De Tomaso (ITALY)

Built by the famous De Tomaso company for 1963, this very attractive Ford powered car was driven by 'Miro Guy' who gained a third at Vallelunga, and by Franco Bernabei who is well remembered for his epic drive at Brands Hatch in the 1963 Anglo-European Trophy Race.

De Tomaso

DB (FRANCE)

Front-engined car with a Panhard engine. At first under powered with the 850 cc engine, this was later replaced by the larger 1100 cc unit. The aluminium bodied cars were front-wheel-drive, and had 5-speed Renault gearboxes.

Delta (GB)

Front-engined car, designed and built by Maurice Phillipe. It had the conventional multi-tubular space frame chassis and was powered by a Ford 105E engine.

Diggory (or Heron) (GB)

Constructed by S J Diggory Motors of Wrexham (see also the Gwyniad), this was a rear-engined car powered by a Ford 105E engine with a multi-tubular frame chassis.

Dolphin (USA)

John Crosthwaite of California designed the Mk 1 Dolphin, known as the Dolphin 'Club'. It was powered by either Fiat or Ford 1100 cc engines, mounted at the rear of the car. The car won first time out, and after a successful 1960 season, the Mk 2 'International' was produced for 1961.

Dolphin (GB)

Not to be confused with the American Dolphin, this was a 'one-off' car was raced by David Latchford (of Halson fame) during the 1960 season. It was powered by a Ford engine.

DRW (GB)

A front-engined car raced regularly by Jack Murrell in 1961. The car was competitive, particularly with Murrell at the wheel who had been successful with the sports car version during the previous year. It was powered by a 997 cc Ford Cosworth engine.

Elfin (AUSTRALIA)

A smart and successful rear-engined car built in Australia by the father and son partnership of Cliff and Garrie Cooper. The cars were raced successfully 'down under' by Arnold Glass and Frank Matich. They were powered by the Ford 105E Cosworth engines, this power being transmitted through Volkswagen 4-speed gearboxes to 13-inch magnesium alloy wheels.

Evad (GB)

Think of the name 'Dave', reverse it, and yes, you have the name of this ex-Monoposto car which was converted to Formula Junior specification. The car was powered by a Ford 998 cc engine, mounted at the front, but was unusual in having wire wheels. David Taylor raced the car regularly throughout 1960.

Ferry (FRANCE)

These rear-engined cars were raced throughout the 1960 season—one of the regular drivers was Yves Dussaud who won at Montlhéry. The cars were powered by a 966 cc Renault engine.

Garford (GB)

This car was built by Gordon Gartside of Harrogate using the parts of F3 500 Cooper. The name is derived from Gartside and the Ford (Cosworth tuned) 105E engine which was mounted at the rear. It had a tubular frame chassis, Cooper suspension units, and a Renault gearbox. The car achieved BTD awards at a number of sprints and hill climbs during 1961.

Gwyniad (GB)

Built by S J Diggory, and raced by Bruce Halford, Chris Meek and George Pitt during 1961. The cars were rear-engined, using the Ford unit and had a tubular space frame chassis. Sometimes known as the Diggory Gwyniad, the cars were designed by Les Redmond, who was also involved with the Gemini and Heron. Only two cars are known to have been built, Diggory selling the cars at the end of the 1961 season. The Gwyniad continued to be raced right up to the end of the Formula Junior era, for Joe Sharps raced a Gwyniad in 1963.

The Gwyniad pictured opposite is Chris Meek's, taken at Oulton Park in the Spring of 1961.

Gwyniad

Halson (GB)

This was recognised as the first British Formula Junior car, and with this 'one-off' car David Latchford became the first British driver to race a British Formula Junior car at International level when he competed in the 1959 Monaco Junior Grand Prix. The Halson was front-engined, powered by a BMC 'A' series unit, bored out to 996 cc, and fitted with a Westlake cylinder head. During 1960 the car was acquired and raced by R Johnson.

Har-Riley (GB)

This car was built for the 1953 Formula 2 and also raced as a 1½-litre Formula 2 car before being fitted with a pre-war 1097 cc Riley 9 engine for Formula Junior. The car was raced by Horace Richards in 1960.

Isis (ITALY)

The Isis was designed and built by Alessandro de Tomaso. It was a rear-engined car, Fiat powered (1100 cc) and looked very similar to the Cooper T52. Suspension was by coil-springs at the front and transverse leaf springs at the rear. The cars were mainly raced in the United States—Harry Heuer and Ron Letellier finishing in third and fourth places at Daytona in 1960.

Jocko Special (USA)

A front-engined car raced by Jim Haynes and designed along Indianapolis lines. The car was Fiat-powered, with a Fiat 4-speed gearbox, and had Borrani wire wheels.

Letchford (GB)

This was a car which was entered by Peter Arundell for J Lisle to drive at Snetterton in October 1960. It had a Ford 997 cc engine.

Mitter (W GERMANY)

Regarded as the most successful Formula Junior car built in West Germany, Gerhard Mitter built and raced this front-engined car during 1959. A number of cars were produced; Carol Shelby drove one in the 1960 Vanderbilt Cup Race. The cars were powered by the 1097 cc 3-cylinder DKW engine.

Opus (GB)

A DKW-powered car raced in 1961 by H E B Mayes. The engine capacity was 980 cc.

PM-Poggi (ITALY)

Sometimes regarded as the Tec Mec Formula Junior car, the Poggi was designed by Ing Massimino and built during the early part of 1959. The chassis is of the tubular ladder type, similar to that of the Stanguellini, and was powered by the Fiat 1100 cc engine, mounted at the front.

Kurt Bardi-Barry drove one of the Poggis during 1960.

Sadler (CANADA)

A front-engined car built by Bill Sadler, of Sadler Cars in Ontario, using BMC components and engine with offset transmission. It had a multi-tubular chassis, aluminum body, and wire wheels. An attractive looking car, almost 'Vanwall' appearance, particularly around the cockpit.

Saxon (GB)

C Scott-MacArthur adapted this Monoposto car to Junior specifications, and raced it in 1959 using a BMC engine, changing this for a DKW unit for the following year. The car was rear-engined, and the power was transmitted via a Volkswagen gearbox. It had a conventional space frame chassis with an alloy body.

Scorpion (GB)

A front-engined car, built by Ryetune of Hastings (which was an associated company of Elva Cars), was produced mainly for the

Scorpion

export market. Ferdinand Konig drove one regularly in this country. Pedro Rodriguez and Chuck Wallace drove Scorpion-DKWs in the United States.

Senior (GB)

A Ford-powered car built by the brothers, David and Douglas Bertram.

Sirmac (FRANCE)

This was a 'one off' car built and raced by Bernard Boyer and was regarded as the most successful French Formula Junior car. Very similar in design to the Ferry cars, it was powered by a Renault engine, mounted at the rear.

Taraschi (ITALY)

A successful Italian car which helped Colin Davis to win the International Championship in 1960, however, it should be said that he also raced the Osca and Stanguellini as well. The Taraschi built for the 1960 season had a tubular ladder-style chassis, was Fiat-powered (the engine was mounted at the front), and had a Fiat 4-speed gearbox. The car was unusual inasmuch as it had a de Dion rear axle.

Venom (GB)

This converted 500 cc Formula Three car with a rear mounted BMC 998 cc engine, was driven successfully by John Fenning during the 1960 season and helped launch him on a successful career within motor racing. Dan Richmond successfully hill climbed the car during 1961.

Venom (front & side profiles)

The Other Formula Juniors

And finally we should not forget the following Formula Juniors:

ITALY	E & W GERMANY	FRANCE
BC	*Bode*	*Dalbot*
BF	*BRW*	*Julien*
Branca	*FRM Tigerjet*	*Rispal*
Conrero	*Hartmann*	*RBS-Simca*
Faccioli	*Liebl*	
Intermeccanica	*Meub*	AUSTRIA
Lippi	*Scampolo*	*MBM*
Lucangeli	*Zimmerman*	*Mathe*
Moretti		*Sauter*
PLW	USA	
Raineri	*BLW*	AUSTRALIA
RAM	*Civet*	*Lambkin*
TecMec	*Dane*	
Wainer	*Elpark*	SWEDEN
	Ocelot	*Saab*

Period Photographs

American Ken Lyon's Lotus-Ford 20 seen in the Goodwood Paddock. He raced the car regularly throughout 1961 with some success, including a win on 10 June at the Goodwood Members' Meeting.

Scotsman Adam Wyllie drove this Lotus-Ford 22 during 1962. It is pictured here at Goodwood during the 1962 Whit-Monday Meeting when it finished in sixth place in the Formula Junior Race.

Malcolm Fruitnight's 1960 Mk 2 Lola-Ford, again in the Goodwood Paddock.

The Scuderia Light Blue Lola-Ford Mk 5 of Hugh Dibley at the 1962 BARC Formula Junior Championship (Goodwood). He finished in ninth place.

Period Photographs

The rear of Ian Raby's Merlyn-Ford Mk 3 at the 1962 Goodwood Whit-Monday Meeting. He finished in fourth place on the road but with a one-minute penalty he was placed further down the field. The car on the right is Hugh Dibley's AC Aceca.

David Prowse's Elva-Auto-Union 100 Series. Note the tilted exhaust.

Another rear—this one is of Mrs B Naylor's Elva-BMC 200 Series at the 1961 Goodwood Whit-Monday Meeting. George Naylor raced the car.

H. Kuderli drove this Mk 3 Gemini-Ford in the 1961 Chichester Cup Race. The car was entered by Scuderia Light Blue. Could this be the same Robert Kuderli who finished third with a Gemini in the E. German Grand Prix in September 1961?

The Deep Sanderson Team (above) with two of the earlier Mk 1 cars and chassis 104 (partly hidden) in the paddock at Oulton Park in August 1960. Note famous Lawrence-prepared Morgan (Reg. TOK 258) next to the Triumph Herald—which has also raced!

Another view of the Deep Sanderson (left), chassis 105, being loaded up on the trailer at Goodwood, September 1962. Len Bridge had driven the car to fourth place in the Formula Junior race.

The MRD drivers Frank Gardner and Gavin Youl (above) taking on fuel of a different nature at the 1962 BARC Formula Junior Championships at Goodwood.

The Brabham Racing Development BT2 seen at the 1962 BARC Formula Junior Championship (Goodwood). Gavin Youl—seen behind the car—finished fifth.

Jo Schlesser's BT6 seen at the Brabham works in 1963 before being shipped to France.

Period Photographs

A tatty but nonetheless intriguing picture of Snetterton, 12 June 1960. The Formula Juniors line up on the grid for the start of a 10 lap race. Front row: car No 39 (far left) is the Lotus 18 of E. L. Hine on pole. He is joined on the front row by the Geminis of Mike Beuttler (44–centre of grid) and Graham Warner (43–far right). Behind on second row is Brian Spicer in the Envoy (38–second from left), and at the start of the third row is the Yimkin.

83

Both Lotus 18s (above) were photographed in the paddock at Goodwood—on the left is Bill Heathcote's dark blue example in September 1961, while on the right is the red and white 18 of the late Rudi De Waldkirch in 1960.

Pictured here (left) is the Farnborough Racing Enterprise Cooper T52 which was driven by M. Bowling at the 1961 Goodwood Whit-Monday Meeting.

Previous page (84) is a marvellous photo typifying the period—David Lockspeiser in his ETA-BMC during the 10 lap Formula Junior race in which he finished eighth, Goodwood, 1 July 1961. Winner of the race was 'Dizzy' Addicott in the Scuderia Light Blue Lola Mk 2.

Formula Juniors in Recent Times

David Grant's 100 Series Elva in which he drove regularly in Historic Formula Junior events, winning the Front-engined Championship in 1990. This Elva has a rather unusual lip on the nose and an additional airbox on the bonnet.

Rob Saunders' Elva 100 Series at Silverstone, April 1983.

Heinz Stege's Elva 100 seen at Zolder, August 1986.

Geoffrey Wragg's Elva-BMC (998 cc) 100 Series at Donington Park, August 1983.

Rob Haze's Cooper T56 at Zolder, August 1986 (above).

John Harper drove this beautiful ex-Ecurie Belge Cooper T67 during 1987 with great success (above right). The car is photographed in the paddock at Castle Combe during August 1987 when John won the joint pre-'65/Formula Junior with ease.

This is the Lola Mk 2 (right) with which Tony Steele has successfully raced in recent years to win the front-engined Historic Championship on a number of occasions, as well as the Championship outright. Interestingly this Lola has both an air intake and carburettor bulge on the bonnet.

Formula Juniors in Recent Times

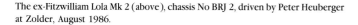

The ex-Fitzwilliam Lola Mk 2 (above), chassis No BRJ 2, driven by Peter Heuberger at Zolder, August 1986.

Frank Tiedeman—a long-time supporter of Historic Formula Junior—is seen here (above right) in his Lotus 22 at Mallory Park in May 1992.

Fredy Kumschick's beautifully prepared Lotus 27 seen here (right) in the paddock at Brands Hatch in 1990 for the Visage Historic Superprix meeting.

Opposite page: Bob Woodward Jnr in his 1962 Cooper T59 at the Chicago Historic Races—Road America, July 1989, and on page 90 Woodward Jnr driving his 1960 Lola Mk 2.

Chris Ball has brought this Lotus 22 (above) back from the USA where he won the 1987 North American Formula Junior Championship with the car. The chassis number is 22J19, one of the ex-Malcolm Templeton cars.

A perfectly restored car by Peter Denty (above right)—this is Dennis Chorley's ex-Ron Harris Lotus 22 seen at Mallory Park in May 1992.

The Northstar as it is today (right) maintained in pristine condition by present owner Martin Cowell, and used by him in hill climb events.

Roger Panter's Envoy (top left) in the 'grassy' paddock of Castle Combe in 1983 at the time when he was racing the Envoy in the Historic Formula Junior Championship.

(Above) The actual Gemini Mk 2 in which Jim Clark made his single-seater début, pictured at Brands Hatch in August 1981.

(Left) This is the ex-Ted Robins' Lotus 20 which was driven by Tony Marsh in 1961, finishing in third place in the 1961 International Trophy Meeting Formula Junior race. The car is now designated a Lotus 20/22 and has been owned for the last 20 years by Mike Murphy who has raced the car often in recent years.

Significant Results 1959 (GB)

19 APRIL – SNETTERTON
First UK race for Formula Junior cars – a Formula Libre event. One Formula Junior car entered, Tommy Dickson (Elva), retired in 2nd heat.

AUGUST BANK HOLIDAY – BRANDS HATCH
Second UK race for Formula Junior cars—mixed with 500cc F3 cars.
1st to 4th places all taken by F3 cars.
5th: Ian Raby (Moorland)

6 SEPTEMBER – CADOURS, FRANCE
The first International Formula Junior race to be won by a British driver with a British car.
1st: Bill de Selincourt (Elva)
2nd: Michael May (Stanguellini)
3rd: Alberti (Stanguellini)
4th: D'Orey (Stanguellini)

4 OCTOBER – BRANDS HATCH
The first race for Formula Junior cars *only* to be held in the UK.
1st: Mike McKee (Elva)
2nd: Bill de Selincourt (Elva)
3rd: Peter Jopp (Elva)
4th: Lawrence (Elva)
Fastest Lap: Bill de Selincourt – 62.4 secs – 71.54 mph.

BOXING DAY BRANDS HATCH FORMULA JUNIOR RACE
1st: Peter Arundell (Elva) – 63.88 mph
2nd: Peter Ashdown (Lola)
3rd: Chris Threlfall (Elva)
4th: Alan Stacey (Lotus 18)
Fastest Lap: Chris Threlfall – 65.45 mph

Significant Results 1959 EUROPE

INTERNATIONAL CHAMPION: Michael May (Stanguellini-Fiat)
ITALIAN CHAMPION: Raffaele Cammarota (Stanguellini-Fiat)
MONACO JUNIOR GP: 1st: Michael May (Stanguellini-Fiat)
2nd: G Alberti (Stanguellini-Fiat)
3rd: Juan M Bordeu (Stanguellini-Fiat)
Fastest Lap: May – 1 min. 54.5 secs – 61.45 mph

Significant Results 1960

BRITISH NATIONAL CHAMPIONSHIP
(Sponsored by *Motor Racing*)
1st: Jimmy Clark and Trevor Taylor (Lotus 18s)
3rd: Mike McKee (Lotus 18)
4th: Peter Arundell (Lotus 18)
5th: John Surtees (Cooper T52)
6th: Dick Prior (Lola Mk 2)

INTERNATIONAL CHAMPIONSHIP
1st: Colin Davis (Osca, Taraschi, and Stanguellini)
2nd: Jacques Cales (Stanguellini)
3rd: Denis Hulme (Cooper T52)
4th: Lorenzo Bandini (Stanguellini)
5th: Henry Grandsire (Stanguellini)
6th: Henry Taylor (Cooper T52)

AMERICAN NATIONAL (SCCA) FORMULA JUNIOR
CHAMPIONSHIP
1st: Charlie Kolb (Elva)

JOHN DAVY CHAMPIONSHIP – BRANDS HATCH
1st: Jimmy Clark (Lotus 18) – 21 points
2nd: Peter Ellis (Lotus 18) – 14 points
3rd: Peter Arundell (Lotus 18) – 13 points

BARC INTERNATIONAL FORMULA JUNIOR CHAMPIONSHIP
– GOODWOOD (August)
1st: Trevor Taylor (Lotus 18) – 90.68 mph
2nd: Jimmy Clark (Lotus 18)

3rd: Mike McKee (Lotus 18)
4th: Dennis Taylor (Lola Mk2)
5th: Peter Ashdown (Lola Mk2)
6th: John Hine (Lotus 18)
Fastest Lap: Taylor and Clark – 92.50 mph

2nd MONACO JUNIOR GRAND PRIX (28 May)
1st: Henry Taylor (Cooper-BMC T52) – 64.52 mph
2nd: Peter Ashdown (Lola-Ford Mk2)
3rd: Trevor Taylor (Lotus-Ford 18)
4th: Peter Arundell (Lotus-Ford 18)
5th: K Lincoln (Cooper-BMC T52)
6th: J Blanc (Cooper-DKW T52)
Fastest Lap: Jimmy Clark (Lotus-Ford 18) – 66.8 mph

LOTTERY GRAND PRIX – MONZA (29 June)
1st: Colin Davis (Osca-Fiat)
2nd: Henri Grandsire (Stanguellini-Fiat)
3rd: Denis Hulme (Cooper-B.M.C.)

SOLITUDE (24 July)
1st: Jimmy Clark (Lotus-Ford 18)
2nd: Steve Ouvaroff (Lotus-Ford 18)
3rd: Trevor Taylor (Lotus-Ford 18)

BRITISH EMPIRE TROPHY RACE – SILVERSTONE
(1 October)
1st: Henry Taylor (Lotus-Ford 18)
2nd: Peter Arundell (Lotus-Ford 18)
3rd: Chuck Dietrich (Elva-BMC 200)

Significant Results 1961

BRITISH NATIONAL CHAMPIONSHIP
(Sponsored by *Motor Racing*)
1st: Trevor Taylor (Lotus 20)

AMERICAN NATIONAL (SCCA) FORMULA JUNIOR
CHAMPIONSHIP
1st: Harry Carter (Lotus-Ford 20)

BARC INTERNATIONAL FORMULA JUNIOR CHAMPIONSHIP
– GOODWOOD (August)
1st: Alan Rees (Lotus 20) – 91.20 mph
2nd: Gavin Youl (MRD-Ford)
3rd: Dennis Taylor (Lola Mk3)
4th: Angus Hyslop (Lotus 20)
5th: Bill Moss (Gemini Mk3)
6th: Mike Spence (Emeryson)
Fastest Lap: Alan Rees – 92.31 mph

3rd MONACO JUNIOR GP (13 May)
1st: Peter Arundell (Lotus-Ford 20)
2nd: John Love (Cooper-BMC)
3rd: Tony Maggs (Cooper-BMC)
4th: Mike McKee (Lotus-Ford 20)
5th: Jo Siffert (Lotus-Ford)
6th: John Hine (Lola-Ford MK3)

PRIX de PARIS – MONTLÉRY (14 May)
1st: Bernard Boyer (Lotus-Ford)
2nd: Robert Bouharde (D.B. Panhard)
3rd: David Piper (Lotus)

GRAND PRIX de FRONTIERES – CHIMAY (21 May)
1st: John Love (Cooper-BMC)
2nd: Tony Maggs (Cooper-BMC)
3rd: Jo Siffert (Lotus-Ford)

LOTTERY GRAND PRIX – MONZA (29 June)
1st: Tony Maggs (Copper-BMC)
2nd: Massimo Natili (Centro-Sud Lotus 20)
3rd: Rob Slotemaker (Lola-Ford)

CIRCUIT OF SOLITUDE
1st: Trevor Taylor (Lotus-Ford 20)
2nd: Peter Arundell (Lotus-Ford 20)
3rd: Tony Maggs (Cooper-BMC T56)
4th: Mike McKee (Lotus-Ford 20)
5th: Gerhard Mitter (Lotus-DKW 18)
6th: Dennis Taylor (Lola MK3)

Significant Results 1962

BRITISH NATIONAL CHAMPIONSHIP
1st: Peter Arundell (Lotus 22)

ITALIAN FORMULA JUNIOR CHAMPIONSHIP
1st: 'Geki' (Lotus 22 and de Sanctis)

AMERICAN NATIONAL FORMULA JUNIOR CHAMPIONSHIP
1st: Tim Mayer (Cooper)

BARC INTERNATIONAL FORMULA JUNIOR CHAMPIONSHIP
– GOODWOOD (August)
1st: Peter Arundell (Lotus 22) – 98.00 mph
2nd: Richard Attwood (Cooper T59)
3rd: Bob Anderson (Lotus 22)
4th: John Fenning (Lola Mk5)
5th: Gavin Youl (Brabham BT2)
6th: John Rhodes (Alexis Mk4)
Fastest Lap: Peter Arundell – 99.08 mph

PRIX DE PARIS – MONTLHÉRY (20 May)
1st: Jo Schlesser (Brabham-Ford) – 70.74 mph
2nd: Robert Bouharde (Cooper-BMC T56)
3rd: Russell Cowles (Cooper-Ford T59)
4th: Robert Kuderli (Cooper-BMC T59)
5th: J. Hampe (DB-Panhard)
6th: Jean Lucienbonnet (Lotus-Ford 20)

4th MONACO JUNIOR GP (2 June)
1st: Peter Arundell (Lotus-Ford 22) – 67.45 mph

2nd: Mike Spence (Lotus-Ford 22)
3rd: Bob Anderson (Lotus-Ford 22)
4th: Kurt Bardi-Barry (Cooper-Ford T59)
5th: C. Manfredini (Wainer-Ford)
6th: 'Geki' (Lotus-Ford 22)

GRAND PRIX DES FRONTIERES – CHIMAY (10 June)
1st: Jose Rosinki (Cooper-Ford T59) – 102.77 mph
2nd: Jo Schlesser (Brabham-Ford)
3rd: John Hine (Lola-Ford Mk5)
4th: Jay Chamberlain (Cooper-BMC T56)
5th: Martin Gould (Lotus-Ford 20)
6th: Teddy Pilette (Merlyn-Ford Mk3)

LOTTERY GRAND PRIX – MONZA (24 June)
1st: Peter Arundell (Lotus-Ford 22) – 113.47 mph
2nd: Alan Rees (Lotus-Ford 22)
3rd: Paul Hawkins (Lotus-Ford 22)
4th: 'Geki' (Lotus-Ford 22)
5th: Tony Maggs (Cooper-BMC T59)
6th: John Love (Cooper-BMC T59)

ALBI GRAND PRIX (9 September)
1st: Peter Arundell (Lotus-Ford 22) – 93.83 mph
2nd: Mike Spence (Lotus-Ford 27)
3rd: Denis Hulme (Cooper-BMC T59)
4th: Jo Schlesser (Brabham-Ford BT2)
5th: Gavin Youl (Brabham-Ford BT2)

Significant Results 1963

BRITISH NATIONAL CHAMPIONSHIP
(Sponsored by *Express and Star* Newspaper)
1st: Peter Arundell (Lotus 27)
2nd: Denis Hulme (Brabham BT6)

AUSTRALIAN FORMULA JUNIOR CHAMPIONSHIP
1st: Leo Geoghegan (Lotus 22)

BARC INTERNATIONAL CHAMPIONSHIP
– GOODWOOD (August)
1st: Peter Arundell (Lotus-Ford 27) – 99.18 mph
2nd: Richard Attwood (Lola-Ford Mk 5A)
3rd: Dennis Hulme (Brabham-Ford BT6)
4th: David Hobbs (Lola-Ford Mk 5A)
5th: John Fenning (Lotus-Ford 27)
6th: Brian Hart (Lotus-Ford 22)
Fastest Lap: Peter Arundell – 100.93 mph

PRIX de PARIS – MONTLHÉRY (19 May)
1st: Frank Gardner (Brabham-Ford)
2nd: Jo Schlesser (Brabham-Ford)
3rd: Peter Revson (Cooper-Ford)

5th MONACO JUNIOR GP (26 May)
1st: Richard Attwood (Lola-Ford Mk 5A) – 69.29 mph
2nd: Frank Gardner (Brabham-Ford BT6)
3rd: Jo Schlesser (Brabham-Ford)
4th: Peter Proctor (Cooper T67)
5th: Bill Bradley (Lola Mk 5A)

6th: 'Geki' (de Sanctis-Ford)
Fastest Lap: Frank Gardner – 113.79 kph (record)

GRAND PRIX des FRONTERIERES – CHIMAY (2 June)
1st: Jacques Maglia (Lotus 22)
2nd: John Ampt (Alexis)
3rd: Jean-Claude Franck (Cooper-Ford)
4th: Robert Bouharde (Cooper-BMC T56)

LOTTERY GRAND PRIX – MONZA (30 June)
1st: Jacques Maglia (Lotus-Ford)
2nd: Colin Davis (Wainer-Ford)
3rd: Kurt Bardi-Barry (Cooper-Ford)

CIRCUIT OF SOLITUDE (28 July)
1st: Peter Arundell (Lotus-Ford 27)
2nd: Dennis Hulme (Brabham-Ford)
3rd: Frank Gardner (Brabham-Ford)
4th: Jo Schlesser (Brabham-Ford)
5th: Richard Attwood (Lola-Ford Mk 5A)
6th: Kurt Ahrens Jnr (Cooper-Ford)

ANGLO-EUROPEAN TROPHY – BRANDS HATCH
(14 September)
1st: Peter Arundell (Lotus-Ford 27) – 91.74 mph
2nd: Denis Hulme (Brabham-Ford)
3rd: Frank Gardner (Brabham-Ford)
4th: Mike Spence (Lotus-Ford 27)

Appendix 1 FORMULA JUNIOR PHOTOGRAPH REFERENCE

Compiled by Alan Putt

CAR	MAGAZINE	DATE	PAGE
Alexis	*Motoring News*	31-Aug-61	11
Alexis	*Autosport*	29-Sep-61	421
Alexis	*Autosport*	29-Sep-61	7
Alexis	*Motoring News*	17-May-62	7
Alexis	*Motoring News*	06-Jun-63	3
Alexis	*Track & Traffic*	01-Apr-62	43
Alexis Mk 2	*Motoring News*	03-Aug-61	9
Apache	*Autocar*	08-Apr-60	581
Apache	*Road & Track*	01-Apr-60	?
Apache	*Sportscar Graphic*	01-Mar-60	23
Apache	*Sportscar Graphic*	01-Mar-60	22
Apache	*Sportscar Graphic*	01-Mar-60	11
Apache Mk 2	*Autosport*	10-Jun-60	787
Arden	*Autosport*	05-Oct-62	468
Ausper	*Autosport*	15-Dec-61	819
Ausper	*Track & Traffic*	01-Apr-62	43
Ausper T2	*Autosport*	30-Dec-60	924
Ausper T3	*Autosport*	06-Oct-61	467
Ausper T3	*Autosport*	13-Oct-61	513
Ausper T3	*Motoring News*	19-Jul-62	8
Ausper T3	*Motoring News*	06-Sep-62	3
Ausper T3	*Vintage Motorsport*	01-Mar-89	25
Ausper T3	*Vintage Motorsport*	01-Mar-89	17
Ausper T4	*Autocar*	04-May-62	738
Ausper T4	*Autosport*	05-Jan-62	16
Ausper T4	*Autosport*	01-Jun-62	790
Ausper T4	*Autosport*	13-Jul-62	41
Ausper T4	*Autosport*	25-Jan-63	120
Ausper T4	*Motoring News*	04-Jan-62	8
Ausper T4	*Motoring News*	31-May-62	5
Ausper T4	*Sporting Motorist*	01-Mar-62	114
Bamosa	*Moteur*	01-Jan-60	28
Bandini	*Vintage Motorsport*	01-Mar-89	16
Bennett	*Motoring News*	22-Sep-60	12
BMD	*Moteur*	01-Jul-59	11
Bode	*Moteur*	01-Jan-60	29
Bode	*Motor Racing*	01-Jun-60	204
Bond	*Autosport*	30-Dec-60	905
Bond	*Autosport*	06-Jan-61	17
Bond	*Classic Car*	01-Apr-90	45
Bougeault	*Victory Lane*	01-Oct-89	14
Brabham BT2	*Autosport*	02-Nov-62	605
Brabham BT2	*Motoring News*	17-May-62	3
Brabham BT2	*Motoring News*	18-Oct-62	12
Brabham BT2	*Autocar*	04-May-62	738
Brabham BT6	*Autosport*	29-Mar-63	420
Brabham BT6	*Autosport*	30-Aug-63	299
Brabham BT6	*Autosport*	22-Nov-63	705
Brabham BT6	*Autosport*	27-Mar-64	419
Brabham BT6	*Autosport*	15-May-64	682
Brabham BT6	*Motoring News*	28-Mar-63	12
Brabham BT6	*Motoring News*	03-May-63	8
Brabham BT6	*Motoring News*	20-Jun-63	5
Brabham BT6	*Victory Lane*	01-Oct-89	52
Britannia	*Autosport*	07-Jul-61	31
BLW	*Road & Track*	01-Apr-60	59
BMC Mk 1	*Vintage Motorsport*	01-Mar-89	16

Appendix 1

CAR	MAGAZINE	DATE	PAGE
BMC Mk 1 (Genie)	*Road & Track*	01-Jul-60	76
Caravelle	*Motor Racing*	01-Oct-60	206
Caravelle	*Track & Traffic*	01-Apr-62	43
Civet	*Motor Racing*	01-Jun-60	204
Condor	*Road & Track*	01-Jul-60	78
Conrero	*Moteur*	01-Jul-59	11
Cooper T52	*Autosport*	24-Jun-60	857
Cooper T52	*Autosport*	24-Jun-60	861
Cooper T52	*Motoring News*	07-Apr-60	7
Cooper T52	*Track & Traffic*	01-Sep-60	29
Cooper T56	*Autosport*	18-Nov-60	700
Cooper T56	*Autosport*	30-Dec-60	905
Cooper T56	*Autosport*	29-Sep-61	427
Cooper T56	*Autosport*	02-Mar-62	318
Cooper T56	*Autosport*	04-Oct-63	471
Cooper T56 & T59	*Autocar*	04-May-62	738
Cooper T59	*Autosport*	05-Jan-62	16
Cooper T59	*Autosport*	10-Aug-62	204
Cooper T59	*Autosport*	31-Aug-62	298
Cooper T59	*Autosport*	14-Sep-62	356
Cooper T59	*Moteur*	01-Jan-62	49
Cooper T59	*Motoring News*	04-Jan-62	1
Cooper T59	*Motoring News*	02-Aug-62	1
Cooper T65	*Moteur*	01-Mar-63	21
Crossle 4S	*Autosport*	08-Jun-62	828
Dagrada	*Moteur*	01-Jul-59	13
Dagrada	*Moteur*	01-Apr-61	21
Dagrada	*Motoring News*	10-Aug-61	9
Dalbot	*Motor Racing*	01-Jun-60	205
Dane	*Motor Racing*	01-Jun-60	205
Dane	*Road & Track*	01-Jul-60	79
De Sanctis	*Autosport*	15-Apr-60	506
De Sanctis	*Moteur*	01-Apr-58	40
De Sanctis	*Moteur*	01-Jul-59	13
De Sanctis	*Moteur*	01-Apr-61	20
De Sanctis	*Sportscar Graphic*	01-Mar-60	15
De Tomaso	*Classic & Sportscar*	01-Aug-86	61
De Tomaso	*Motor Racing*	01-Jan-63	467
De Tomaso	*Motoring News*	03-Aug-61	8
De Tomaso	*Vintage Motorsport*	01-Mar-89	17
De Tomaso-Ford	*Autosport*	20-Sep-63	388
Deep Sanderson	*Autosport*	15-Apr-60	507
Deep Sanderson	*Autosport*	02-Sep-60	331
Deep Sanderson	*Autosport*	06-Jan-61	17
Deep Sanderson	*Classic Car*	01-Apr-90	47
Deep Sanderson	*Motoring News*	05-Jan-61	8
Degrada	*Vintage Motorsport*	01-Mar-89	16
Dolphin	*Autosport*	14-Apr-61	482
Dolphin (F/E GB)	*Autosport*	07-Oct-60	513
DRW	*Classic Car*	01-Apr-90	47
DRW	*Motor*	01-Feb-61	38
DRW	*Motoring News*	16-Feb-61	6
Elfin Mk 1 (GB)	*Autocar*	07-Oct-60	558
Elfin Mk 1 (GB)	*Autosport*	11-Nov-60	668
Elfin Mk 1 (GB)	*Motor*	09-Nov-60	588
Elfin Mk 1 (GB)	*Motor Racing*	01-Dec-60	354
Elfin Mk 2 (GB)	*Autosport*	09-Nov-62	638

Appendix 1

CAR	MAGAZINE	DATE	PAGE
Elfin Mk 2 (GB)	*Small Car*	01-Feb-63	51
Elfin Mk 2 (GB)	*Small Car*	01-Feb-63	53
Elfin Mk 2 (GB)	*Small Car*	01-Feb-63	52
Elfin (Australian)	*Autosport*	21-Dec-62	840
Elfin (Australian)	*Autosport*	21-Jun-63	863
Elfin (Australian)	*Motor Racing*	01-Jan-63	479
Elfin (Australian)	*Motoring News*	09-Nov-61	9
Elva	*Autosport*	01-Jul-60	22
Elva	*Autosport*	26-May-61	690
Elva	*Classic Car*	01-Apr-90	45
Elva	*Motoring News*	20-Aug-59	11
Elva	*Motoring News*	31-Dec-59	1
Elva	*Motoring News*	07-Jan-60	6
Elva	*Track & Traffic*	01-Sep-60	26
Elva	*Track & Traffic*	01-Sep-60	27
Elva	*Vintage Motorsport*	01-Mar-89	17
Elva Mk 2	*Moteur*	01-Jan-61	25
Elva Mk 2	*Motor Racing*	01-Nov-60	283
Elva Mk 3	*Autosport*	30-Dec-60	906
Elva Mk 3	*Autosport*	26-Jan-62	124
Elva Mk 3	*Autosport*	25-Jan-63	118
Elva Mk 3	*Moteur*	01-Jan-62	51
Elva Mk 3	*Motoring News*	25-May-61	5
Elva Mk 3	*Motoring News*	18-Apr-63	5
Elva Mk 3	*Sporting Motorist*	01-Mar-62	115
Elva Mk 3	*Victory Lane*	01-Oct-89	58
Elva Mk 3	*Track & Traffic*	01-Apr-62	42
Elva Mk 3	*Vintage Motorsport*	01-Mar-89	24
Emeryson	*Autosport*	02-Sep-60	322
Emeryson	*Moteur*	01-Jan-61	25
Emeryson	*Motoring News*	01-Sep-60	1
Emeryson	*Motoring News*	05-Jan-61	8
Emeryson	*Motoring News*	03-Aug-61	8
Emeryson	*Track & Traffic*	01-Apr-62	42
Envoy	*Autosport*	04-Oct-63	468
Envoy	*Classic Car*	01-Apr-90	42
Envoy	*Track & Traffic*	01-Sep-60	29
Evad	*Motor Racing*	01-Jun-60	205
Faccioli	*Moteur*	01-Jan-60	22
Faccioli	*Road & Track*	01-Apr-60	65
Faccioli	*Sportscar Graphic*	01-Mar-60	17
Fergusson	*Track & Traffic*	01-Sep-60	30
Ferry	*Autocar*	08-Apr-60	579
Ferry	*Moteur*	01-Jul-59	10
Ferry	*Motor Racing*	01-Jun-59	191
Filippi-Morini	*Moteur*	01-Apr-58	40
Filippi-Morini	*Moteur*	01-Apr-58	38
Foglietti	*Moteur*	01-Jul-59	12
Foglietti	*Moteur*	01-Apr-61	20
Garford	*Autosport*	15-Dec-61	811
Garford	*Motor Racing*	01-Aug-60	206
Garford	*Motoring News*	09-Jun-60	9
Gemini	*Motoring News*	20-Aug-59	10
Gemini	*Motoring News*	31-Dec-59	7
Gemini	*Motoring News*	07-Apr-60	8
Gemini Mk 2	*Classic Car*	01-Apr-90	47
Gemini Mk 2	*Classic Car*	01-Apr-90	45

Appendix 1

CAR	MAGAZINE	DATE	PAGE
Gemini Mk 2	*Sportscar Graphic*	01-Mar-60	15
Gemini Mk 2	*Track & Traffic*	01-Sep-60	29
Gemini Mk 2	*Vintage Motorsport*	01-Mar-89	17
Gemini Mk 3	*Autosport*	19-Aug-60	265
Gemini Mk 3	*Autosport*	30-Dec-60	890
Gemini Mk 3	*Motoring News*	11-Aug-60	9
Gemini Mk 3a	*Autosport*	12-Jan-62	57
Gemini Mk 3a	*Autosport*	19-Jan-62	93
Gemini Mk 3a	*Motoring News*	31-Aug-61	5
Gemini Mk 3a	*Road & Track*	01-Jul-61	83
Gemini Mk 3a	*Track & Traffic*	01-Apr-62	42
Gemini Mk 4	*Autosport*	27-Apr-62	590
Gemini Mk 4	*Autosport*	01-Jun-62	790
Gemini Mk 4	*Motoring News*	05-Apr-62	1
Gemini Mk 4	*Motoring News*	04-Oct-62	5
Gemini Mk 4	*Motoring News*	12-Sep-63	1
Gemini Mk 4	*Victory Lane*	01-Oct-89	51
Gemini Mk 4a	*Autosport*	13-Sep-63	351
Gemini Mk 4a	*Autosport*	13-Sep-63	352
Gemini Mk 4a	*Motor Racing*	01-Mar-63	89
Halson	*Autosport*	07-Aug-59	189
Halson	*Classic Car*	01-Apr-90	47
Halson	*Moteur*	01-Jul-59	11
HAR	*Motoring News*	15-Sep-60	12
Hartmann	*Moteur*	01-Jan-60	29
Hartmann	*Motor Racing*	01-Jun-60	203
Hartmann	*Motor Rundschau*	05-Aug-59	560
Heron	*Autosport*	09-Dec-60	798
Heron	*Autosport*	07-Apr-61	431
Heron	*Autosport*	08-Sep-61	327
Heron	*Motoring News*	25-May-61	12
Intermeccanica	*Motor Racing*	01-Jun-60	204
ISIS	*Motor Racing*	01-Dec-60	389
ISIS	*Motor Racing*	01-Jan-60	192
ISIS	*Motor Racing*	01-May-60	154
ISIS	*Motor Racing*	01-Jun-60	20
ISIS	*Road & Track*	01-Apr-60	54
ISIS	*Victory Lane*	01-Oct-89	32
Kieft	*Track & Traffic*	01-Apr-62	43
Kieft	*Vintage Motorsport*	01-Mar-89	20
Liebl	*Motor Racing*	01-Jun-60	205
Lola	*Motoring News*	07-Jan-60	6
Lola Mk 2	*Autosport*	22-Jul-60	129
Lola Mk 2	*Autosport*	12-Aug-60	233
Lola Mk 2	*Autosport*	26-Aug-60	301
Lola Mk 2	*Motoring News*	31-Dec-59	1
Lola Mk 2	*Track & Traffic*	01-Sep-60	27
Lola Mk 2	*Victory Lane*	01-Oct-89	58
Lola Mk 2	*Victory Lane*	01-Oct-89	57
Lola Mk 3	*Autosport*	24-Feb-61	231
Lola Mk 3	*Classic Car*	01-Apr-90	43
Lola Mk 3	*Track & Traffic*	01-Apr-62	42
Lola Mk 3	*Track & Traffic*	01-Apr-62	42
Lola Mk 5	*Autosport*	30-Mar-62	451
Lola Mk 5	*Autosport*	30-Mar-62	450
Lola Mk 5	*Autosport*	15-Jun-62	870
Lola Mk 5	*Autosport*	06-Jul-62	8

Appendix 1

CAR	MAGAZINE	DATE	PAGE
Lola Mk 5	*Autosport*	17-May-63	679
Lola Mk 5	*Autosport*	14-Jun-63	825
Lola Mk 5	*Motoring News*	29-Mar-62	3
Lola Mk 5	*Vintage Motorsport*	01-Mar-89	17
Lola Mk 5a	*Autosport*	13-Sep-63	351
Lola Mk 5a	*Motor Racing*	01-Mar-63	89
Lola Mk 5a	*Motoring News*	23-May-63	3
Lola Mk 5a	*Motoring News*	05-Sep-63	5
Lotus 18	*Autosport*	15-Jul-60	89
Lotus 18	*Autosport*	19-Aug-60	253
Lotus 18	*Autosport*	02-Sep-60	326
Lotus 18	*Autosport*	30-Dec-60	905
Lotus 18	*Autosport*	13-Oct-61	514
Lotus 18	*Autosport*	21-Dec-62	853
Lotus 18	*Autosport*	26-Jul-63	136
Lotus 18	*Classic Car*	01-Apr-90	43
Lotus 18	*Motoring News*	07-Jan-60	6
Lotus 18	*Motoring News*	07-Apr-60	12
Lotus 18	*Track & Traffic*	01-Sep-60	27
Lotus 18	*DKW Autosport*	04-Nov-60	648
Lotus 20	*Autosport*	08-Sep-61	327
Lotus 20	*Autosport*	29-Sep-61	427
Lotus 20	*Autosport*	13-Oct-61	516
Lotus 20	*Autosport*	08-Jun-62	829
Lotus 20	*Autosport*	02-Aug-63	155
Lotus 20	*Moteur*	01-Jan-61	24
Lotus 20	*Track & Traffic*	01-Apr-62	42
Lotus 22	*Autosport*	04-May-62	625
Lotus 22	*Autosport*	24-Aug-62	264
Lotus 22	*Autosport*	12-Jul-63	69
Lotus 22	*Moteur*	01-Jan-62	51
Lotus 22	*Motoring News*	04-Jan-62	1
Lotus 22	*Victory Lane*	01-Oct-89	52
Lotus 22	*Victory Lane*	01-Oct-89	54
Lotus 22 (Costin)	*Autosport*	11-Oct-63	493
Lotus 27	*Autosport*	01-Feb-63	150
Lotus 27	*Autosport*	13-Mar-64	338
Lotus 27	*Autosport*	27-Mar-64	419
Lotus 27	*Moteur*	01-Mar-63	21
Lotus 27	*Motor Racing*	01-Mar-63	86
Lotus 27	*Motoring News*	31-Jan-63	1
Lotus 27	*Motoring News*	01-Aug-63	12
Lynx	*Motoring News*	19-Apr-62	9
Machan	*Road & Track*	01-Jul-60	79
Mallock U2	*Motoring News*	26-Jul-62	9
Mathe	*Motor Racing*	01-Jun-60	206
Melkus	*Autosport*	15-Apr-60	506
Melkus	*Moteur*	01-Jan-60	29
Melkus	*Motor Racing*	01-Jun-60	203
Merlyn Mk 3	*Autosport*	04-Aug-61	151
Merlyn Mk 3	*Autosport*	05-Jan-62	9
Merlyn Mk 3	*Autosport*	25-May-62	735
Merlyn Mk 3	*Autosport*	25-Jan-63	117
Merlyn Mk 3	*Moteur*	01-Jan-62	50
Merlyn MK 3	*Motoring News*	04-Jan-62	7
Merlyn Mk 3	*Motoring News*	06-Dec-62	9
Merlyn Mk 3	*Sporting Motorist*	01-Mar-62	115

Appendix 1

CAR	MAGAZINE	DATE	PAGE
Merlyn Mk 5	Autosport	15-Feb-63	217
Merlyn Mk 5	Moteur	01-Mar-63	21
Merlyn Mk 5	Motoring News	24-Jan-63	4
Merlyn Mk 5	Victory Lane	01-Oct-89	56
Mitter	Autocar	08-Apr-60	579
Mitter	Moteur	01-Jan-60	29
Mitter	Motor Racing	01-Jun-60	204
Mitter	Motor Rundschau	25-Jun-59	404
Mitter	Road & Track	01-Jul-60	78
Mitter	Sportscar Graphic	01-Mar-60	15
Momomill	Classic Car	01-Apr-90	43
Monomill	Moteur	01-Jul-59	10
Monomill	Motor Racing	01-Jun-60	203
Monomill	Motoring News	08-Oct-59	12
Moorland	Autosport	24-Apr-59	518
Moorland	Motor Racing	01-Sep-59	192
Moorland	Vintage Motorsport	01-Mar-89	16
Moretti	Moteur	01-Jul-59	13
Moretti	Moteur	01-Apr-61	20
Moretti	Road & Track	01-Apr-60	61
Moretti	Road & Track	01-Jul-61	90
MRD	Autosport	25-Aug-61	260
MRD	Autosport	08-Sep-61	315
MRD	Classic & Sportscar	01-Aug-86	61
MBM	Autosport	18-Mar-60	367
MBM	Motor Racing	01-Jun-60	154
MBM	Motoring News	17-Mar-60	10
MBM	Motoring News	04-Jan-62	7
MBM	Motoring News	22-Mar-62	9
MRD	Track & Traffic	01-Apr-62	43
North Star	Autosport	13-Sep-63	348
Nota	Sports Car World	01-Jul-60	63
OSCA	Moteur	01-Apr-61	21
OSCA	Sportscar Graphic	01-Mar-60	16
OSCA	Sportscar Graphic	01-Mar-60	17
OSCA	Vintage Motorsport	01-Mar-89	16
Poggi	Autosport	11-Dec-59	761
Poggi	Autosport	15-Apr-60	506
Poggi	Motor Racing	01-Jun-59	435
Poggi	Road & Track	01-Apr-60	60
Poggi-Tec-Mec	Motor Racing	01-Jun-60	204
Puzey	Autosport	25-May-62	735
Rainieri	Sportscar Graphic	01-Mar-60	15
Rispal	Moteur	01-Jul-59	11
Rispal	Motor Racing	01-Jun-59	190
Saab	Autosport	09-Feb-62	203
Saab	Car & Driver	01-Aug-61	61
Saab	Motoring News	27-Oct-60	8
Sadler	Road & Track	01-Apr-60	54
Sadler	Track & Traffic	01-Sep-60	30
Sadler	Vintage Motorsport	01-Mar-89	23
Sadler	Vintage Motorsport	01-Mar-89	17
Sauter	Motor Racing	01-Jun-60	204
Saxon	Autosport	10-Jul-59	43
Saxon	Motor	15-Apr-59	396
Saxon	Motor Racing	01-Jun-60	204
Saxon	Sportscar Graphic	01-Mar-60	14

CAR	MAGAZINE	DATE	PAGE
Sirmac	Moteur	01-Jul-60	76
Stanguellini	Autosport	20-Mar-59	367
Stanguellini	Classic Car	01-Apr-90	43
Stanguellini	Classic Car	01-Apr-90	45
Stanguellini	Moteur	01-Jul-59	12
Stanguellini	Moteur	01-Apr-61	21
Stanguellini	Motoring News	26-Mar-59	10
Stanguellini	Motoring News	31-Mar-60	12
Stanguellini	Sportscar Graphic	01-Mar-60	15
Stanguellini	Sportscar Graphic	01-Mar-60	13
Stanguellini	Sportscar Graphic	01-Mar-60	12
Stanguellini	Track & Traffic	01-Sep-60	29
Stanguellini Mk 1	Victory Lane	01-Oct-89	26
Stanguellini Mk 2	Autosport	03-Nov-61	628
Stanguellini Mk 2	Autosport	24-Nov-61	719
Stanguellini Mk 2	Autosport	13-Mar-64	338
Stanguellini Mk 2	Motor Racing	01-Dec-61	427
Stanguellini Mk 2	Sporting Motorist	01-Mar-62	115
Stanguellini (Prototype)	Autosport	29-Nov-57	691
Stebro Mk 4	Victory Lane	01-Oct-89	60
Stebro Mk 4	Victory Lane	01-Oct-89	59
Stebro Mk 4	Vintage Motorsport	01-Mar-89	23
Taraschi	Autocar	08-Apr-60	581
Taraschi	Moteur	01-Jul-59	12
Taraschi	Moteur	01-Apr-61	21
Taraschi	Motor Racing	01-Jun-59	424
Taraschi	Road & Track	01-Apr-60	56
Taraschi	Sportscar Graphic	01-Mar-60	25
Taraschi	Sportscar Graphic	01-Mar-60	24
Taraschi	Sportscar Graphic	01-Mar-60	10
Taraschi	Sportscar Graphic	01-Mar-60	24
Taraschi	Vintage Motorsport	01-Mar-89	21
Taraschi (Giuar)	Autosport	15-Apr-60	507
Terrier	Autosport	13-Oct-61	501
Terrier	Autosport	26-Jan-62	123
Terrier	Autosport	07-Sep-62	321
Terrier	Classic & Sportscar	01-Aug-86	61
Terrier	Motor Racing	01-Jun-60	204
Tomahawk	Motor Racing	01-Dec-60	424
TCA	Autosport	23-Dec-60	882
TCA	Motor Racing	01-Jun-60	203
Virgo	Autosport	16-Oct-59	509
Volpini	Autosport	15-Apr-60	506
Volpini	Moteur	01-Jul-59	12
Volpini	Motor Racing	01-Jun-60	203
Volpini	Road & Track	01-Apr-60	55
Wainer	Classic Car	01-Apr-90	47
Wainer	Moteur	01-Jul-59	13
Wainer	Moteur	01-Apr-61	20
Wainer	Road & Track	01-Jul-60	77
Wainer	Vintage Motorsport	01-Mar-89	16
Wainer-Ford	Autosport	21-Sep-62	391
Wainer-Ford	Autosport	01-Feb-63	163
Wainer-Monteverdi	Motor	15-Apr-59	396
Yimkin	Autosport	15-Apr-60	507
Yimkin	Motor Racing	01-Jun-60	206
Zimmerman	Moteur	01-Jan-60	29
Zimmerman	Motor Racing	01-Jun-60	205

Appendix 2 FORMULA JUNIOR ARTICLES REFERENCE

Compiled by Alan Putt

ARTICLE	SUBJECT	MAGAZINE	DATE	PAGE
Alexis	Car	*Motor*	24-Feb-60	124
Alexis	Car	*Autocar*	26-Feb-60	340
Alexis	Car	*Motoring News*	03-Mar-60	10
Alexis	Car	*Motoring News*	21-Jul-60	9
Alexis	Car	*Motor*	18-Apr-62	413
Alexis-DAF (Drawing)	Car	*Motor*	05-Jun-65	41
Alexis Mk1 to Mk 18	Car	*Autosport*	20-Dec-68	20
Andree; F.Jnr Lab.	Car	*Motor Life*	01-Apr-61	53
Apache	Car	*Motoring News*	02-Jul-59	6
Ausper	Car	*Aust. Motor Sport*	01-Apr-61	136
Ausper, Australia's	Car	*Sports Car World*	10-Feb-62	?
Ausper T3	Car	*Autosport*	15-Dec-61	818
Ausper T3	Car	*Motor*	03-Jan-62	877
Ausper T3	Car	*Motor Racing*	01-Feb-62	53
Bandini (Track Test)	Car	*Grid*	01-Oct-60	54
BMC	Car	*Road & Track*	01-Jul-60	76
BMC Mk 2	Car	*Road & Track*	01-Dec-61	104
BMC (Track Test)	Car	*Sports Car Graphic*	01-Jun-61	62
Bond	Car	*Motor*	14-Dec-60	764
Bond	Car	*Motoring News*	15-Dec-60	1
Bond	Car	*Autocar*	16-Dec-60	1045
Bond	Car	*Autosport*	16-Dec-60	?
Bond	Car	*Motor Racing*	01-Feb-61	55
Bond	Car	*Motor*	01-Feb-61	38
Bond (Track Test)	Car	*Motor Racing*	01-Mar-61	96
Bourgeault (sketch)	Car	*Car & Driver*	01-Aug-61	44
Brabham, MRD history	Car	*Autosport*	15-Nov-68	26
Brabham, P.w.Junior	Car	*Motor Racing*	01-May-62	161
Brabham BT2	Car	*Autocar*	?	404
Brabham BT2	Car	*Motor*	21-Mar-62	254
Brabham BT2	Car	*Autosport*	24-Mar-62	420
Brabham BT2	Car	*Autocar*	04-May-62	738
Brabham BT2	Car	*Sports Car Graphic*	01-Jul-62	30
Brabham BT2 Dev.	Car	*Motor Racing*	01-Jun-62	206
Brabham BT2 (T.Test)	Car	*Motor Racing*	01-May-62	163
Brabham BT6	Car	*Motor*	15-May-63	46
Brabham BT6 (Sketch)	Car	*Autosport*	08-Mar-63	324
Brabham (MRD)	Car	*Autosport*	01-Sep-61	282
Brabham (MRD)	Car	*Motor Racing*	01-Dec-61	428
Brabham (MRD)	Car	*Road & Track*	01-Jan-62	28
Britannia	Car	*Autocar*	11-Mar-60	428
Britannia	Car	*Autocar*	06-May-60	745
Britannia	Car	*Autosport*	06-May-60	606
Britannia	Car	*Motor*	11-May-60	578
Britannia	Car	*Motoring News*	12-May-60	1
Britannia	Car	*Autosport*	22-Sep-61	387
Brittania	Car	*Motoring News*	05-Dec-60	1
BMC (Genie)	Car	*Road & Track*	01-Feb-64	78
BMC (Genie) Mk 2	Car	*Road & Track*	01-Dec-61	104
BMC (Genie) Mk 6	Car	*SCI*	01-Jun-63	60
Condor	Car	*Autosport*	19-Feb-60	228
Condor	Car	*Motor*	24-Feb-60	124
Condor	Car	*Autocar*	26-Feb-60	340
Condor	Car	*Motor Racing*	01-May-60	96
Condor	Car	*Road & Track*	01-Jul-60	78
Conrero	Car	*Moteur*	01-Apr-59	18
Conrero (Drawing)	Car	*Moteur*	01-Jan-60	22

ARTICLE	SUBJECT	MAGAZINE	DATE	PAGE
Cooper, The Story	Car	*Autosport*	03-Jan-69	22
Cooper Race Plans	Car	*Motoring News*	26-Feb-59	10
Cooper T52	Car	*Autocar*	06-Nov-59	588
Cooper T52	Car	*Motoring News*	19-Nov-59	12
Cooper T52	Car	*Cars Illustrated*	01-Jul-60	236
Cooper T52 (Sketch)	Car	*Motor*	11-Nov-59	530
Cooper T52 (Sketch)	Car	*Moteur*	01-Jan-60	23
Cooper T56	Car	*Motoring News*	17-Nov-60	1
Cooper T56	Car	*Road & Track*	01-Mar-61	85
Cooper T56	Car	*Autosport*	02-Feb-62	153
Cooper T56 (Sketch)	Car	*Motor*	19-Apr-61	429
Cooper T59	Car	*Motor*	03-Jan-62	879
Cooper T59	Car	*Autocar*	04-May-62	738
Cooper T59 (Sketch)	Car	*Autocar*	02-Feb-62	180
Cooper T67	Car	*Car & Driver*	01-May-62	79
Cooper T67	Car	*Autosport*	25-Jan-63	107
Cooper T67	Car	*Motor*	15-May-63	46
Cooper T67 (illust.)	Car	*Autosport*	01-Feb-63	160
Dagrada (illust.)	Car	*Car & Driver*	01-Aug-61	48
Dagrada (Track Test)	Car	*SCI*	01-Sep-60	28
Dane	Car	*Road & Track*	01-Jul-60	79
DB Panhard (illust.)	Car	*Motoring News*	15-Jun-61	9
DB (illust.)	Car	*Moteur*	01-Apr-61	22
De Tomaso	Car	*Auto Italiana*	13-Dec-62	?
De Tomaso	Car	*Autosport*	04-Jan-63	6
Deep Sanderson	Car	*Motoring News*	25-Feb-60	10
Deep Sanderson	Car	*Motoring News*	21-Jul-60	9
Delfin (Czech)(illust.)	Car	*Automobil*	01-Mar-64	2
Diggory Gwiniad	Car	(see Heron)		
Dolphin	Car	*Motor*	07-Dec-60	728
Dolphin	Car	*Motor*	10-May-61	556
Dolphin Mk1 (illust.)	Car	*SCI*	01-Dec-60	38
Dolphin Mk2 (illust.)	Car	*Car & Driver*	01-Aug-61	38
DRW (Track Test)	Car	*Motoring News*	16-Feb-61	6
DRW	Car	*Motor*	01-Feb-61	38
Elfin (Australian)	Car	*Austrl. Motor Sport*	01-Nov-62	16
Elfin (Australian)	Car	*Motor Racing*	01-Jan-63	479
Elfin (Australian) Itself	Car	*Sports Car World*	01-May-69	20
Elfin (Australian) Part 2	Car	*Sports Car World*	01-Aug-61	30
Elfin (Australian) Story	Car	*Sports Car World*	01-May-69	16
Elfin (Australian)	Car	*Sports Car World*	01-Jul-62	11
Elfin (Australian)	Car	*Sports Car World*	01-Jan-62	8
Elfin (British)	Car	*Motor*	09-Nov-60	589
Elfin (British)	Car	*Autosport*	11-Nov-60	668
Elfin (British)	Car	*Motor Racing*	01-Dec-60	424
Elfin (British)	Car	*Autosport*	09-Nov-62	638
Elfin (British)	Car	*Small Car*	01-Feb-63	51
Elva	Car	*Motor*	02-Dec-59	632
Elva	Car	*Autocar*	04-Dec-59	738
Elva	Car	*Moteur*	01-Jan-60	24
Elva, A Visit to	Car	*Motoring News*	25-Jan-62	3
Elva, Junior	Car	*Motoring News*	05-Feb-59	10
Elva Mk 2	Car	*Motor Racing*	01-Nov-60	389
Elva Mk 2	Car	*Motoring News*	08-Sep-60	9
Elva Mk 2	Car	*Motoring News*	06-Oct-60	9
Elva Mk 2	Car	*Autosport*	07-Oct-60	491
Elva Mk 2	Car	*Motor*	12-Oct-60	382

Appendix 2

ARTICLE	SUBJECT	MAGAZINE	DATE	PAGE
Elva Mk 2	Car	*Motor*	19-Apr-61	429
Elva Mk 2 (Track Test)	Car	*Autosport*	04-Nov-60	638
Elva Mk 3	Car	*Autosport*	01-Dec-61	750
Elva Mk 3	Car	*Motor*	06-Dec-61	765
Elva Mk 3	Car	*Motor*	03-Jan-62	876
Elva Mk 3	Car	*Autocar*	04-May-62	738
Elva Story Part 1	Car	*Autosport*	19-Nov-65	?
Elva Story Part 2	Car	*Autosport*	26-Nov-65	868
Elva (Drawing)	Car	*Motor Racing*	01-Sep-59	312
Elva (Drawing)	Car	*Motor Racing*	01-Jun-60	199
Elva (Track Test)	Car	*Autosport*	01-Jan-60	?
Elva (Track Test)	Car	*Road & Track*	01-Jun-60	43
Elva-DKW (Track Test)	Car	*Motoring News*	31-Mar-60	8
Emeryson	Car	*Motoring News*	21-Jul-60	9
Emeryson	Car	*Motor*	31-Aug-60	142
Emeryson	Car	*Autosport*	02-Sep-60	?
Emeryson	Car	*Motoring News*	17-Nov-60	8
Envoy	Car	*Motor*	13-Jan-60	835
Envoy	Car	*Motor*	03-Feb-60	10
Envoy	Car	*Autosport*	05-Feb-60	?
Envoy	Car	*Autocar*	05-Feb-60	235
Envoy	Car	*Cars Illustrated*	01-Mar-60	336
Envoy (Track Test)	Car	*Motoring News*	25-Feb-60	8
Envoy (Track Test)	Car	*Road & Track*	01-Feb-61	41
Envoy — Racing at Junior prices	Car	*Austl. Motor Sport*	01-Apr-60	134
Ferry	Car	*Autosport*	24-Jul-59	101
Ferry	Car	*Moteur*	01-Jan-60	30
Ferry (Drawing)	Car	*Moteur*	01-Jan-59	35
Ferry (Drawing)	Car	*Autosport*	01-May-59	554
Ferry (Drawing)	Car	*Moteur*	01-Jul-59	14
Focus Mk 4	Car	*Motoring News*	22-Nov-62	9
Garford	Car	*Motor*	25-May-60	659
Gemini	Car	*Motoring News*	13-Aug-59	10
Gemini, More Gen on the	Car	*Motoring News*	27-Aug-59	10
Gemini, At the Sign of the Cheq. Flag	Car	*Motor Sport*	01-May-60	335
Gemini Mk 2	Car	*Moteur*	01-Jan-60	26
Gemini Mk 2	Car	*Motor*	10-Feb-60	52
Gemini Mk 2 (illust.)	Car	*Autosport*	08-Jan-60	48
Gemini Mk 2 (Track Test)	Car	*Cars Illustrated*	01-Jan-60	234
Gemini Mk 3	Car	*Motor*	31-Aug-60	145
Gemini Mk 3	Car	*Motor*	16-Nov-60	622
Gemini Mk 3	Car	*Motor*	19-Apr-61	429
Gemini Mk 3a (Track Test)	Car	*Motor Racing*	01-Feb-61	53
Gemini Mk 3a (Track Test)	Car	*Motoring News*	09-Feb-61	6
Gemini Mk 4	Car	*Motor Racing*	01-Feb-62	60
Gemini Mk 4	Car	*Autosport*	23-Mar-62	405
Gemini Mk 4	Car	*Autocar*	04-May-62	738
Gemini Mk 4	Car	*Road & Track*	01-Jun-62	78
Gemini Mk 4	Car	*Autosport*	25-Jan-63	107
Gemini Mk 4 (illust.)	Car	*Motor*	28-May-62	266
Gemini Mk 4a	Car	*Autocar*	04-May-62	738
Gemini Mk 4a	Car	*Motoring News*	17-Jan-63	9
Gemini Mk 4a	Car	*Motor*	15-May-63	46
Gemini Story Part 1	Car	*Motor Racing*	01-Feb-62	61
Gemini Story Part 2	Car	*Motor Racing*	01-Mar-62	108
Gemini, Cheq. Flag Pt 1	Car	*Autosport*	01-Apr-60	424
Gemini, Cheq. Flag Pt 1	Car	*Autosport*	12-Jan-62	53

ARTICLE	SUBJECT	MAGAZINE	DATE	PAGE
Gemini, Cheq. Flag Pt 2	Car	*Autosport*	08-Apr-60	469
Gemini, Cheq. Flag Pt 2	Car	*Autosport*	19-Jan-62	92
Gemini, Cheq. Flag Pt 3	Car	*Autosport*	29-Apr-60	579
Hartmann	Car	*Motor*	13-Apr-60	400
Heron	Car	*Autosport*	25-Nov-60	733
Heron	Car	*Autosport*	23-Dec-60	860
Heron	Car	*Autosport*	07-Apr-61	431
Hillwood	Car	*Motor*	24-May-61	631
Jocko Special	Car	*Autosport*	15-Apr-60	508
Jolus, Evolution of	Car	*Sports Car World*	1-Feb-62	?
Kieft	Car	*Motoring News*	16-Mar-61	3
Kieft	Car	*Motor*	21-Sep-60	245
Kieft (Track Test)	Car	*Autosport*	17-Mar-61	348
Kieft (Track Test)	Car	*Motor Sport*	01-Apr-61	262
Kieft (Track Test)	Car	*Motoring News*	20-Apr-61	6
Lambkin	Car	*Sports Car World*	01-Jun-60	44
Lippi	Car	*Autocar*	13-Nov-59	631
Lola makes its Mark	Car	*Victory Lane*	01-Oct-89	57
Lola Mk 2	Car	*Moteur*	01-Jan-60	26
Lola Mk 2	Car	*Victory Lane*	01-Oct-89	57
Lola Mk 2	Car	*Autocar*	18-Dec-59	806
Lola Mk 2	Car	*Autosport*	18-Dec-59	793
Lola Mk 2 (Drawing)	Car	*Motor*	30-Dec-59	783
Lola Mk 3	Car	*Motor*	22-Feb-61	129
Lola Mk 3	Car	*Motor Racing*	01-Mar-61	101
Lola Mk 3	Car	*Motor*	19-Apr-61	429
Lola Mk 3	Car	*Motoring News*	21-Feb-62	3
Lola Mk 3 (Drawing)	Car	*Motor*	15-Feb-61	82
Lola Mk 3 (Drawing)	Car	*Motor*	15-Feb-61	82
Lola Mk 3 (Drawing)	Car	*Autosport*	28-Apr-61	544
Lola Mk 3 (Drawing)	Car	*Car & Driver*	01-Aug-61	42
Lola Mk 5 (Track Test)	Car	*Motor Racing*	01-Jun-62	212
Lola Mk 5a	Car	*Motor*	15-May-63	46
Lola Mk 5a (Drawing)	Car	*Autosport*	27-Dec-63	869
Lotus 18	Car	*Motoring News*	17-Dec-59	5
Lotus 18	Car	*Moteur*	01-Jan-60	25
Lotus 18	Car	*Motor*	20-Jan-60	868
Lotus 18	Car	*Road & Track*	01-Mar-61	85
Lotus 18 (Drawing)	Car	*Autosport*	29-Apr-60	580
Lotus 18 (Track Test)	Car	*Motoring News*	25-Feb-60	9
Lotus 18 (Drawing)	Car	*Autocar*	01-Jan-60	12
Lotus 20	Car	*Motoring News*	05-Jan-61	1
Lotus 20	Car	*Motor Racing*	01-Feb-61	54
Lotus 20	Car	*Road & Track*	01-Apr-61	50
Lotus 20	Car	*Motor*	19-Apr-61	429
Lotus 20 (Drawing)	Car	*Motor*	08-Feb-61	54
Lotus 20 (Drawing)	Car	*Autosport*	24-Mar-61	376
Lotus 20 (Drawing)	Car	*Road & Track*	01-Aug-61	48
Lotus 20 (Track Test)	Car	*Motor*	01-Mar-61	162
Lotus 20 (Track Test)	Car	*Motoring News*	02-Mar-61	6
Lotus 20 (Track Test)	Car	*Autosport*	03-Mar-61	268
Lotus 20 (Track Test)	Car	*Motor Racing*	01-Apr-61	130
Lotus 20 (Track Test)	Car	*Road & Track*	01-Aug-61	46
Lotus 22	Car	*Motor*	03-Jan-62	879
Lotus 22	Car	*Autosport*	05-Jan-62	20
Lotus 22	Car	*Autosport*	09-Feb-62	194
Lotus 22	Car	*Car & Driver*	01-May-62	78

Appendix 2

ARTICLE	SUBJECT	MAGAZINE	DATE	PAGE
Lotus 22 (Drawing)	Car	*Car & Driver*	01-Oct-62	47
Lotus 22 (Track Test)	Car	*Motoring News*	08-Feb-62	3
Lotus 22 (Track Test)	Car	*Motor Racing*	01-Mar-62	90
Lotus 27	Car	*Motor*	15-May-63	46
Lotus 27 (Drawing)	Car	*Autosport*	22-Feb-63	260
Lynx	Car	*Motoring News*	19-Apr-62	9
Lynx, New Lower, Lighter	Car	*Austrl. Motor Sport*	01-Sep-62	46
Lynx-Borgward, Victorias	Car	*Austrl. Autosport*		?
Lynx-Borgward (Track T.)	Car	*Aust. Autosportmn.*	01-Jan-64	19
Lynx-Ford; Bruce Powell's (T.T.)	Car	*Sports Car World*	01-Jun-62	24
Lynx; Latest Line Up Pt1	Car	*Sports Car World*	01-Nov-61	25
Lynx; Latest Line Up Pt2	Car	*Sports Car World*	01-Dec-61	28
Machan	Car	*Road & Track*	01-Jul-60	79
Mallock U2	Car	*Bulletin, 750*	01-Oct-61	?
Mallock U2	Car	*Motor Racing*	01-Apr-62	146
Mallock U2	Car	*Small Car*	01-Nov-62	40
Mallock U2 Poor Man Racing	Car	*Motor Sport*	01-Mar-61	146
Merlyn, Colchester Racing Dev.	Car	*Autosport*	22-Nov-68	24
Merlyn Mk 1	Car	*Autosport*	09-Dec-60	?
Merlyn Mk 2	Car	*Motoring News*	04-May-61	1
Merlyn Mk 2	Car	*Motor*	17-May-61	586
Merlyn Mk 3	Car	*Motoring News*	04-May-61	797
Merlyn Mk 3	Car	*Motoring News*	20-Jul-61	9
Merlyn Mk 3	Car	*Motor*	09-Aug-61	586
Merlyn Mk 3 (Track Test)	Car	*Motor Racing*	01-Feb-62	9
Mitter	Car	*Road & Track*	01-Jul-60	78
MBM	Car	*Motor*	16-Mar-60	67
Nami Moskovitch	Car	Autosport	17-Feb-61	70
Nota	Car	*Austrl. Motor Sport*	01-Jun-63	221
Osca (illust.)	Car	*Moteur*	01-Jan-60	20
Raineri	Car	*Autosport*	23-Dec-60	882
Saab	Car	*Motoring News*	20-Oct-60	1
Saab	Car	*Motor*	26-Oct-60	529
Saab	Car	*Autosport*	04-Nov-60	?
Sadler, Junior by	Car	*Motoring News*	11-Feb-60	10
Sadler (illust.)	Car	*Grid*	01-Aug-60	35
Sadler (illust.)	Car	*Autocourse*	01-Sep-60	6
Stanguellini Mk 2 (illus)	Car	*Car & Driver*	01-May-62	72
Stanguellini Mk 2	Car	*Motor*	18-Oct-61	476
Stanguellini Mk 2	Car	*Motoring News*	16-Nov-61	9
Stanguellini Mk 2	Car	*Autosport*	24-Nov-61	719
Stanguellini (illust.)	Car	*Motor*	24-Feb-60	719
Stanguellini (Drawing)	Car	*Motor Racing*	01-Jul-60	476
TCA; Ultimate DKW Junior	Car	*SCI*	01-Aug-60	60
TCA; Trips mit einem neuen Junior	Car	*Auto Motor u Sport*	21-May-60	38
Tojeiro -		see Britannia		
TCA (Drawing)	Car	*Motor Racing*	01-Jun-60	201
Valour (NZ)	Car	*Autosport*	15-Mar-63	356
Venom	Car	*Motor Sport*	01-Oct-61	862
Volpini (Track Test)	Car	*SCI*	01-Sep-60	201
Wainer	Car	*Road & Track*	01-Jul-60	77
Wainer (Track Test)	Car	*SCI*	01-Sep-60	28
Transistor Ignition	Engine	*Motor Life*	01-Apr-61	50
BMC A Series Engine	Engine	*Motor Sport*	01-May-64	349
DKW Juniors	Engine	*SCI*	01-Aug-60	57
Ford Engines	Engine	*Motor Sport*	01-Aug-64	34
FJ Engines for 1962 P1	Engine	*Autosport*	15-Dec-61	815

Appendix 2

Appendix 2

In case of difficulty in obtaining a Bookmarque title please write for a
catalogue and further information, enclosing a S.A.E to:
Bookmarque Publishing
26 Cotswold Close · Minster Lovell · Oxfordshire OX8 5SX.